Sounds

of

Emptiness

Sounds of Emptiness

by

Todd Lorentz

Vedanta Publishing

Edmonton, Canada

Sounds of Emptiness

by Todd Lorentz

ISBN: 978-0-9877782-4-6

Printed in the United States of America.

First Edition, February 2019

Published by Vedanta Publishing
Edmonton, Canada
www.VedantaPublishing.com

Dedicated to Maitreya,
The World Teacher

Forward

Humanity is entering a period of unprecedented spiritual growth and we are facing questions at this time regarding the very nature and purpose of our existence here on planet earth. Who are we? Why are we here? Is there some Plan or Purpose for our existence that relates to our very nature and spiritual essence? Apart from many significant spiritual cycles which *do* mark this present time as an especially transformative period in humanity's spiritual evolution, we have also brought upon ourselves calamitous material outcomes and circumstances from living on this planet as if there were no consequences for our activities. While every substantial spiritual teaching through all history has warned that we will always reap the results of the seeds that we sow from our actions (otherwise known as *Karma*) we continue to disregard any concern for the actual working out of that principle.

Frighteningly, we have brought our continued existence on this planet into question and already witness the onset of tipping points from which we will likely never be able to recover. In the environment, we are witnessing the recent messages of distress regarding the demise of whole biological chains of life which threaten the stability of entire global forest systems, the impending death of most coral reefs around the world, the dramatic and fatal shift in ocean acidity, the cascading collapse of the world's glacial systems, the onset of meteorological extremes and much more. Politically speaking, global relations have largely broken down giving way to mistrust, cynicism, suspicion, authoritarianism and fascism, racism, bigotry and massive corruption. In the economic sphere we now participate rather despondently in a callous and fraudulent system geared entirely to enriching a very few entitled individuals while virtually most of the remaining population of the earth face stagnation at best and starvation at the worst. Religion worldwide has increasingly failed its mandate to provide relevant spiritual instruction and monotonously reassures those who can still tolerate the exclusiveness and intolerance which has grown like weeds in the garden of modern discourse. This terminally toxic promise of salvation endures while various leaders of religious institutions uphold their message amidst scandals of congregational abuse or deliver their discourses assuming the superiority of their particular doctrine. For humanity, this has resulted in a world cynical of government, untrusting of science, disillusioned by religion, morally confused, financially bankrupt and somewhat stranded on the shores of history with no clear direction for the future. At least in our common global bewilderment we can say that we were united in some sort of mutual planetary suffering.

This brings me to the motivation for creating this book of meditations. In the midst of the world's present struggle, the need for self-examination in order to find some greater truth about ourselves is paramount. Quite simply, our collective view of life and reality is mistaken and has led to the disastrous situation that we find in the world today. We live within One united and integrated Whole yet we operate in the world "as if" we are entirely separate and disconnected from one another. The result has been enormously destructive throughout the ages. Granted, the appearance of the "form" world to our physical senses certainly seems to imply some sort of material separation between us and our fellow travellers. However, the greatest spiritual traditions in history – now increasingly corroborated by such fields as quantum physics and studies in the nature of consciousness – have helped us to understand more about the true nature of reality as One. Behind the façade of outer physical appearances we discover a livingness within all of us that is deeply integrated and interconnected. We now persist in this folly of separation at our very peril and the only way forward out of sure extinction is to bring our entire attention to understanding the nature of life and our place within it. The meditations that I have gathered together here are not new and have been said before in a multitude of ways. But I have hopefully made them accessible to the reader in a manner that invites their contemplation and understanding. In them, if pondered and expanded upon, lies the solution to our present crisis as well as our future growth.

I have also chosen to illustrate this book using my own black and white imagery gathered along my travels. The activity of the mind has the curious characteristic of viewing all input through the lens of memory and existing beliefs. Therefore, when we see a colour image – which is similar to how our visual senses take in the world – our mind will immediately bring to bear a memory, an idea or a viewpoint through which to identify and process that image. By presenting the same view in black and white the mind has, if only very briefly, no immediate recognition and must sit stunned for a moment while evaluating the image based on its composite shapes and forms. It is in this space between thoughts, this moment of temporary conceptual suspension, that the mind has access to that larger field of consciousness behind individual identity. In a flash of insight or moment of intuition one can penetrate beyond the sensory world of familiar forms. This is where reality truly lives and where we need to look in order to find our way forward into the future.

The general level of human consciousness and knowledge makes it possible for a great leap forward by humanity at this time. We are now collectively capable of understanding that we are part of One Cosmos, and capable of re-ordering our lives in a way that will conform to that vision and end the destruction and ruin of our world. Toward this I offer my small book of meditations.

Todd Lorentz
January, 2019

For those who wish to climb the mountain of spiritual awareness, the path is selfless work.

For those who have attained the summit of union with the Lord, the path is stillness and peace.

– *The Bhagavad Gita*

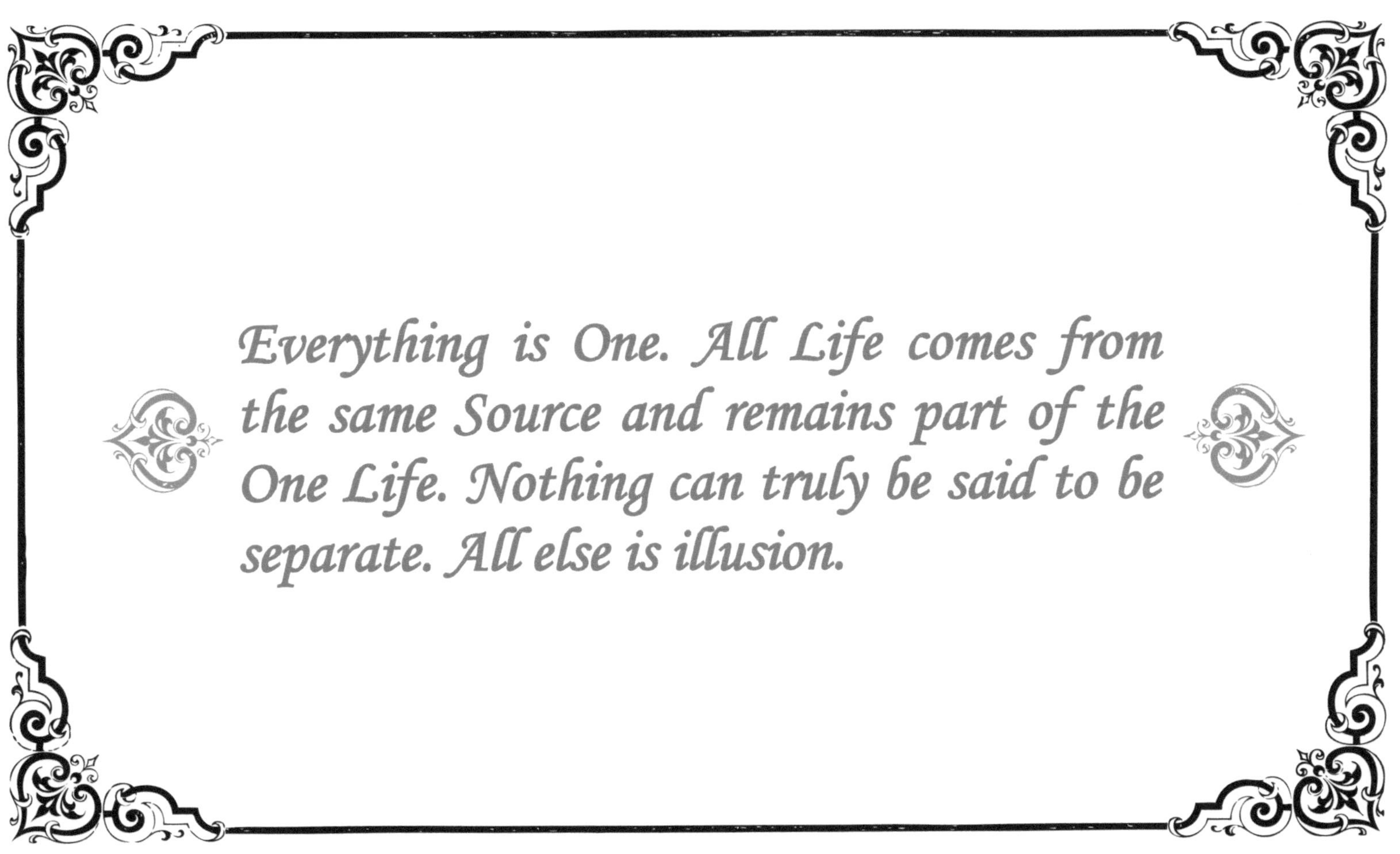

Everything is One. All Life comes from the same Source and remains part of the One Life. Nothing can truly be said to be separate. All else is illusion.

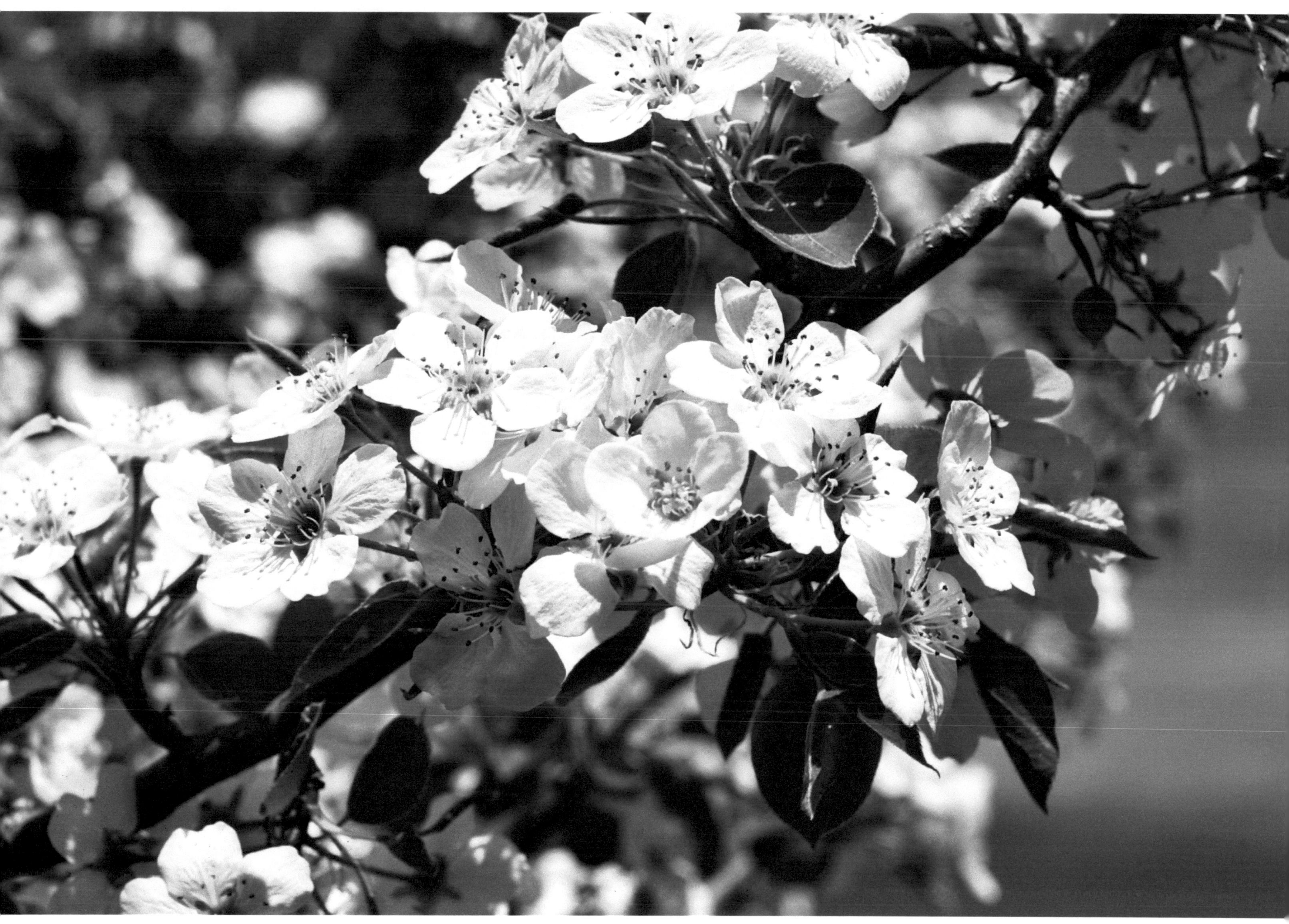

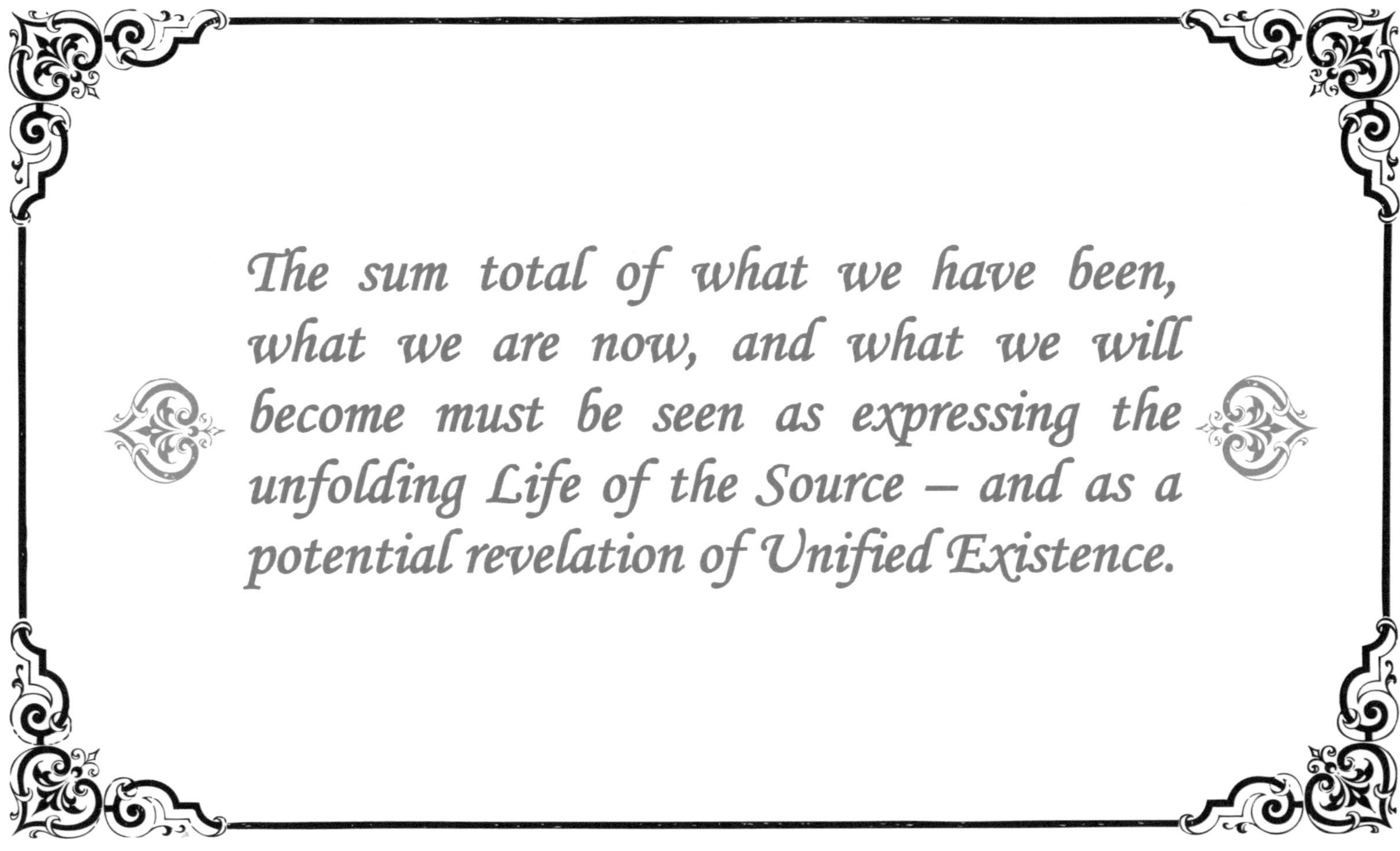

The sum total of what we have been, what we are now, and what we will become must be seen as expressing the unfolding Life of the Source – and as a potential revelation of Unified Existence.

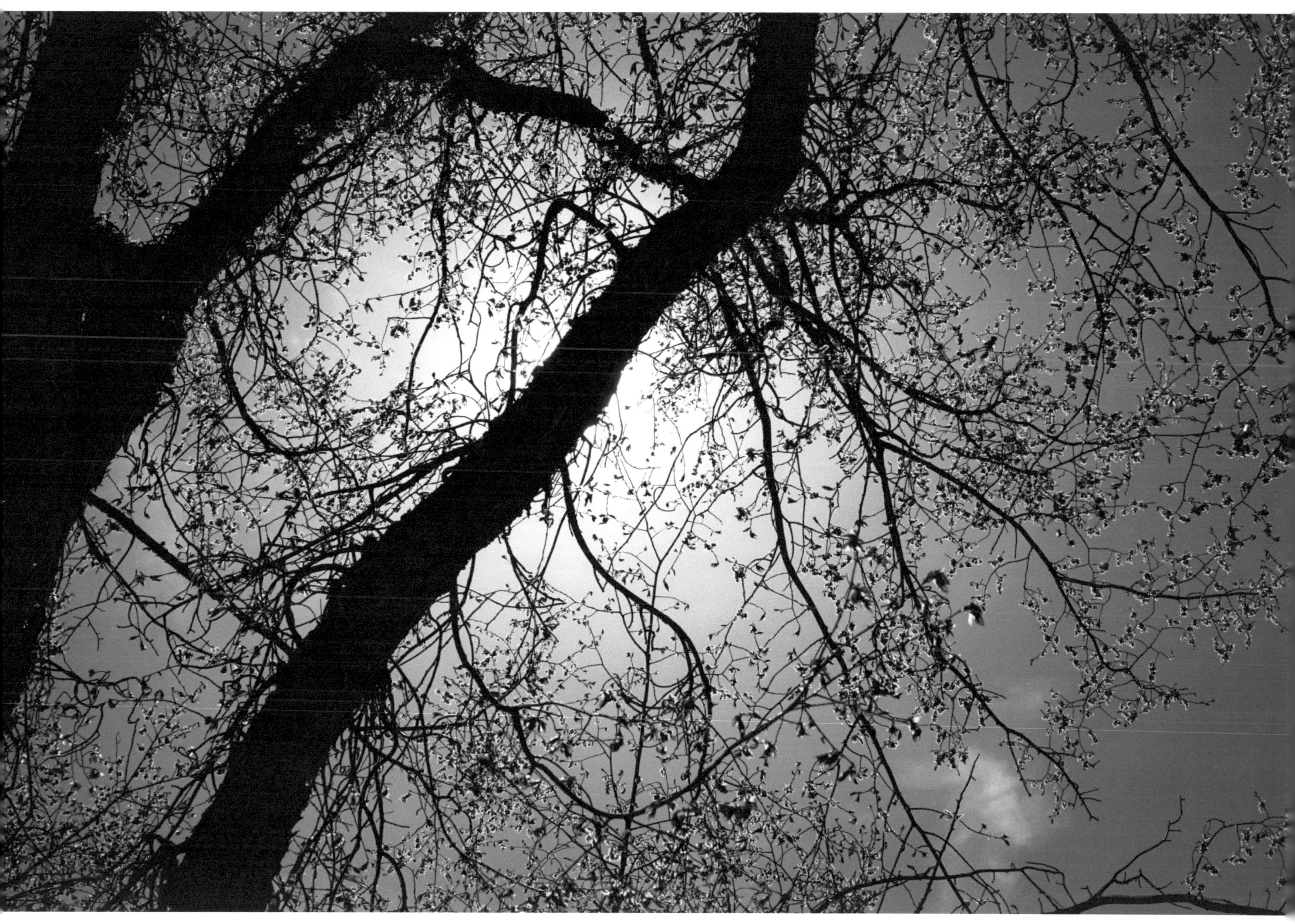

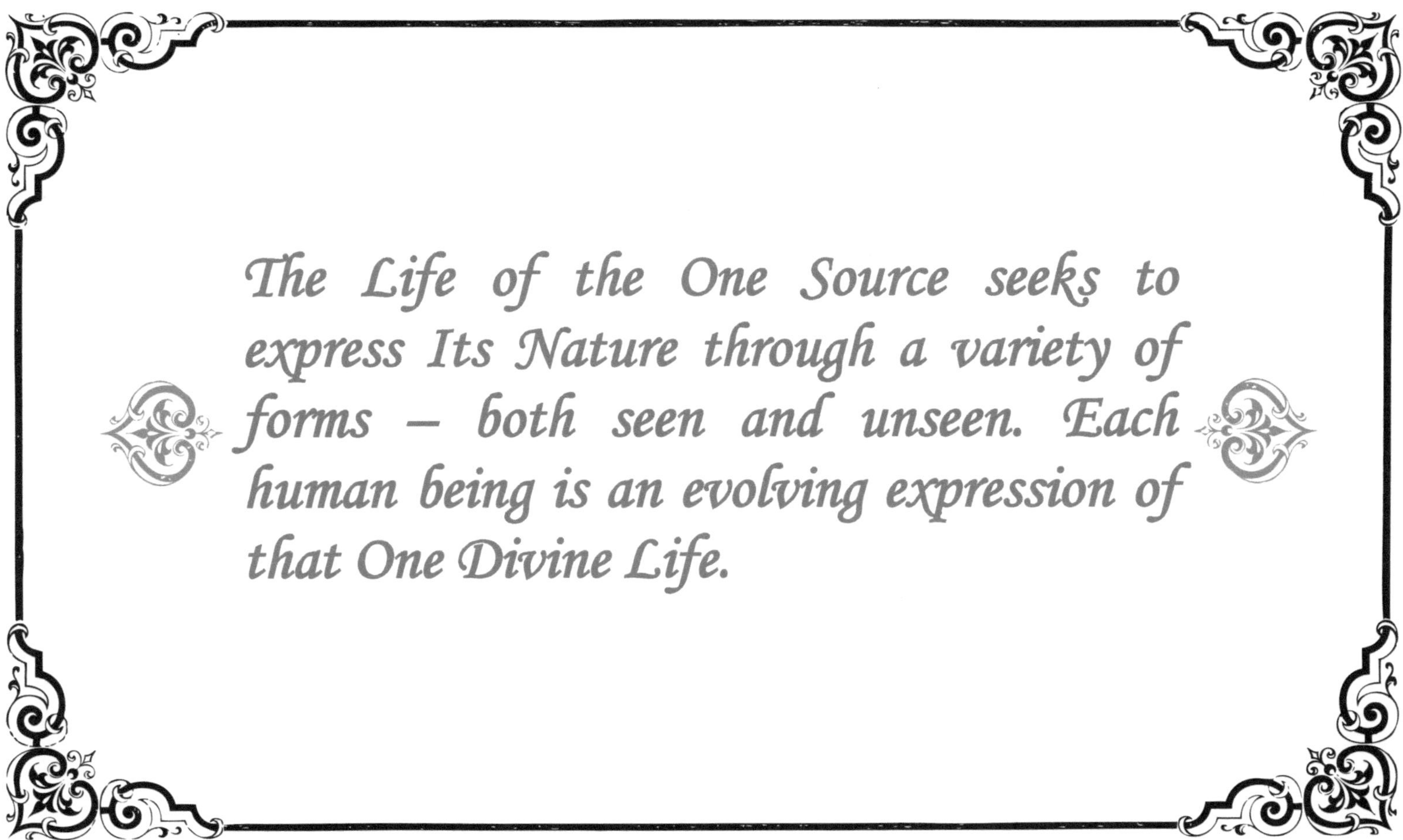

The Life of the One Source seeks to express Its Nature through a variety of forms – both seen and unseen. Each human being is an evolving expression of that One Divine Life.

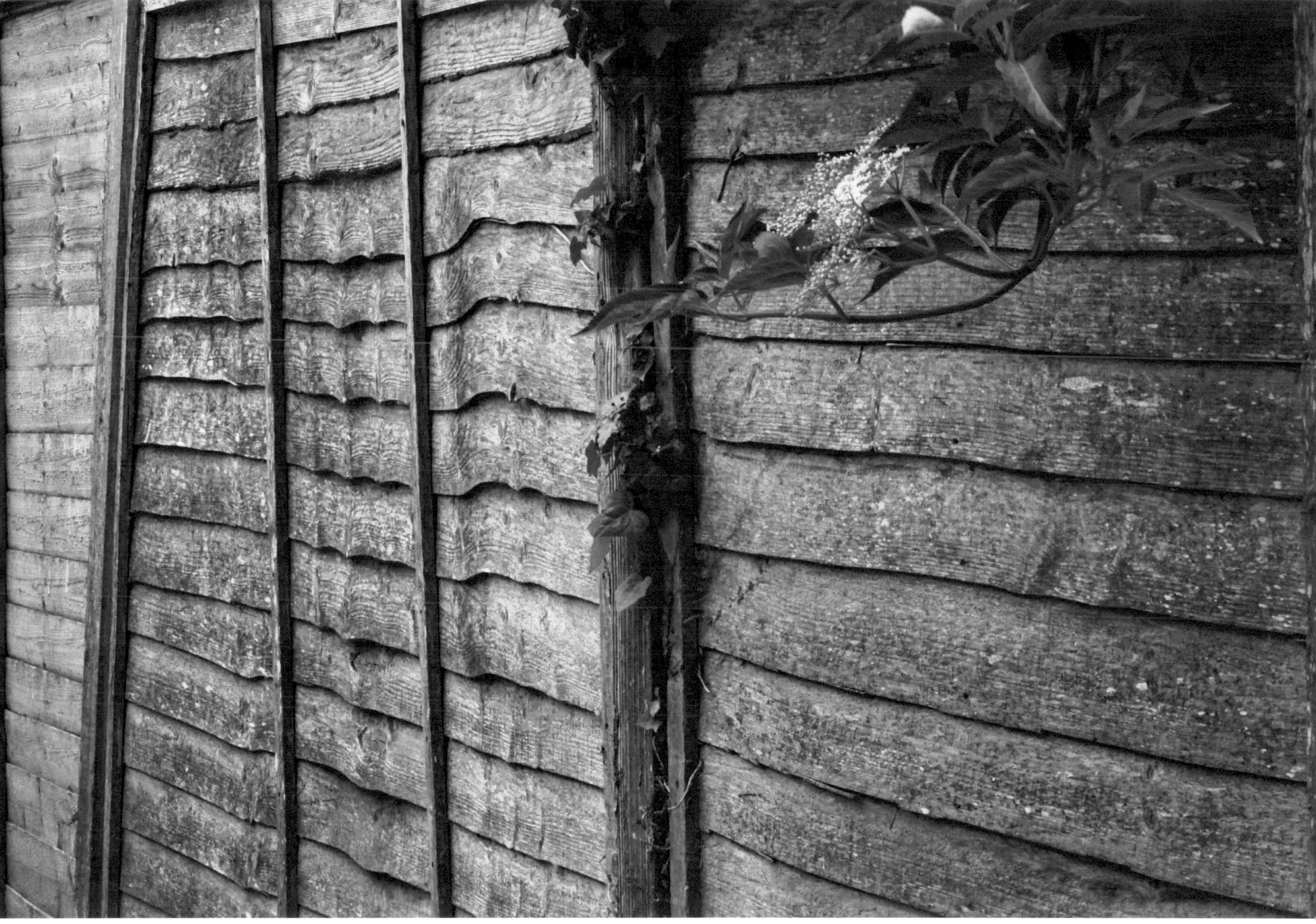

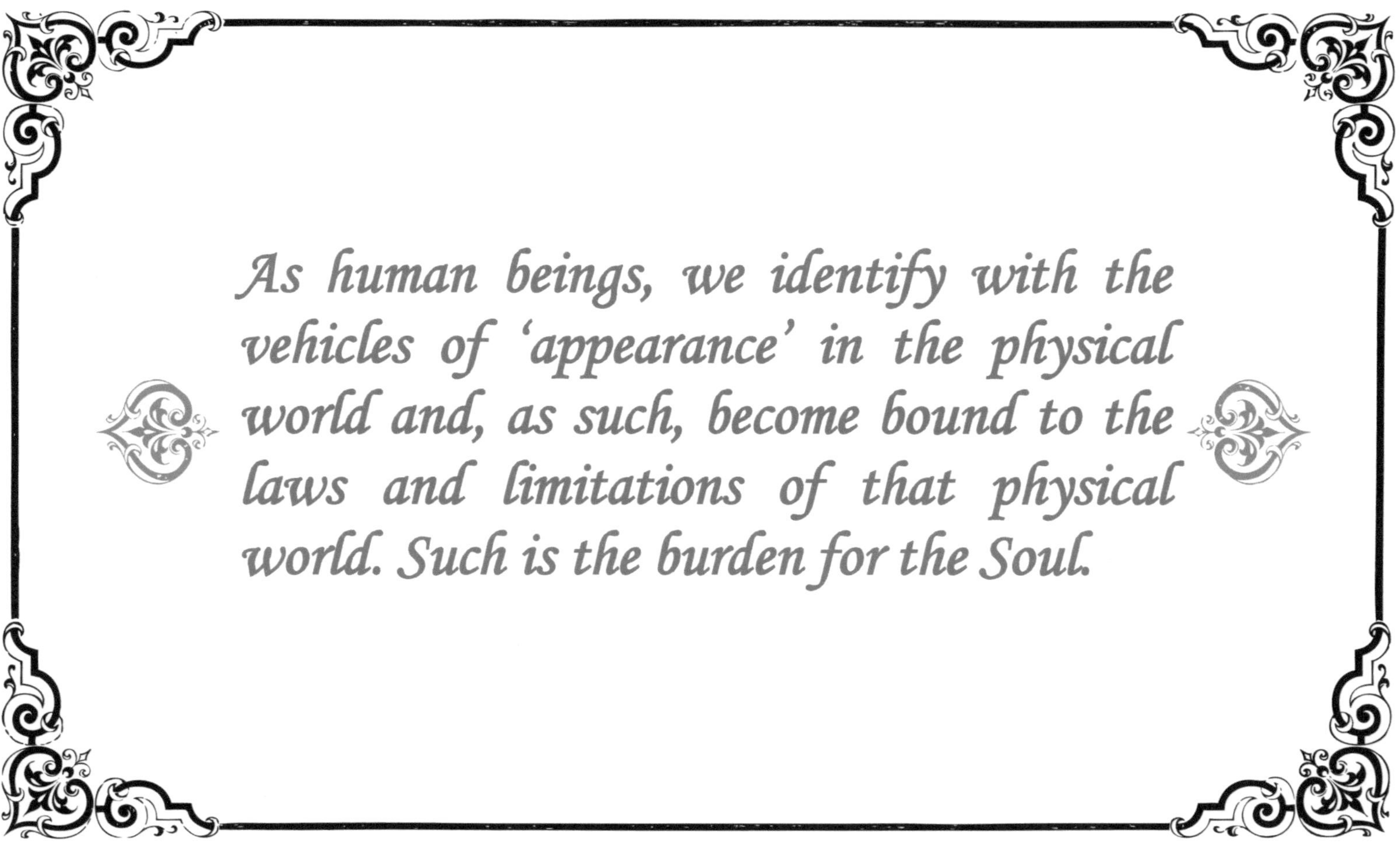

As human beings, we identify with the vehicles of 'appearance' in the physical world and, as such, become bound to the laws and limitations of that physical world. Such is the burden for the Soul.

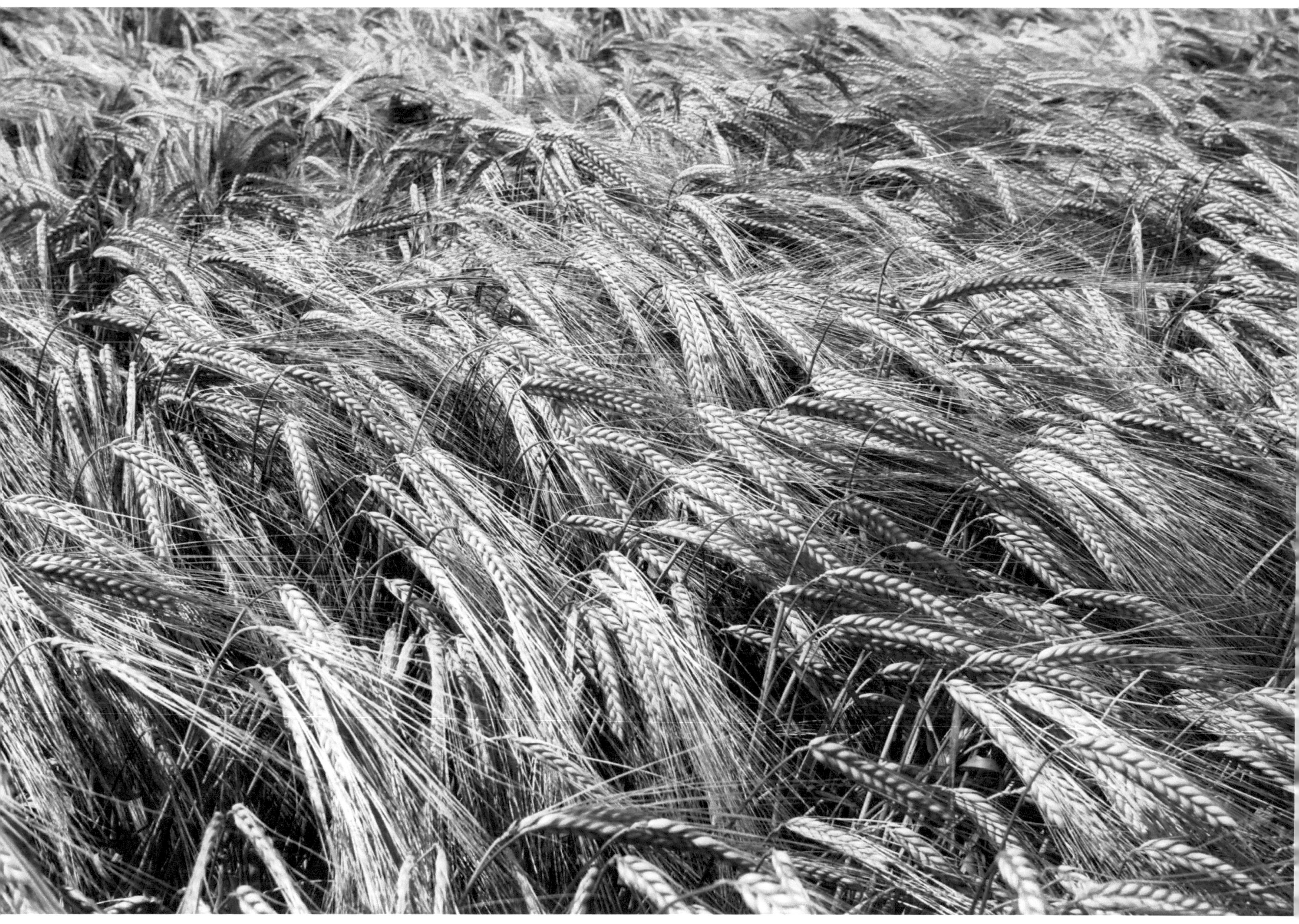

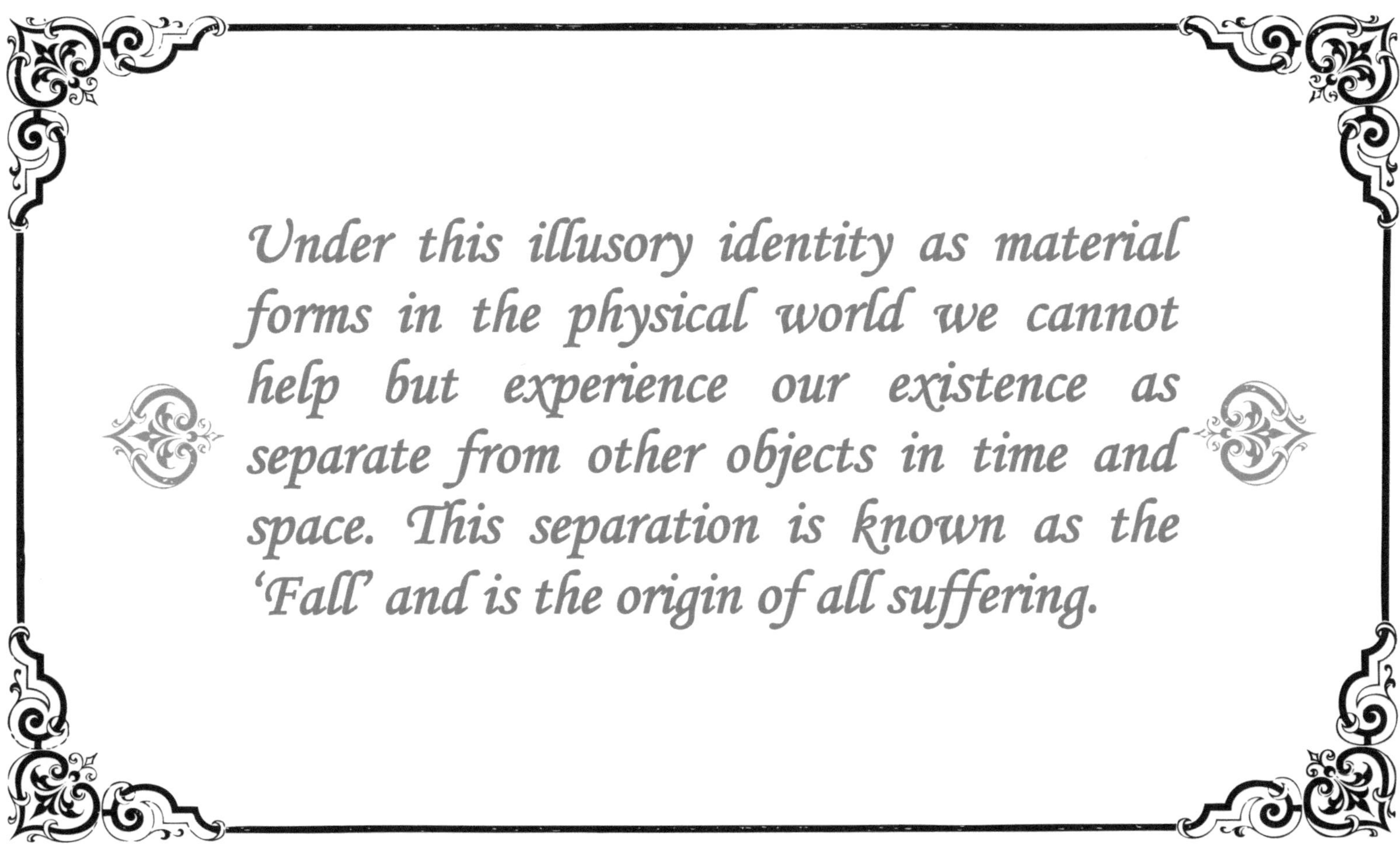

Under this illusory identity as material forms in the physical world we cannot help but experience our existence as separate from other objects in time and space. This separation is known as the 'Fall' and is the origin of all suffering.

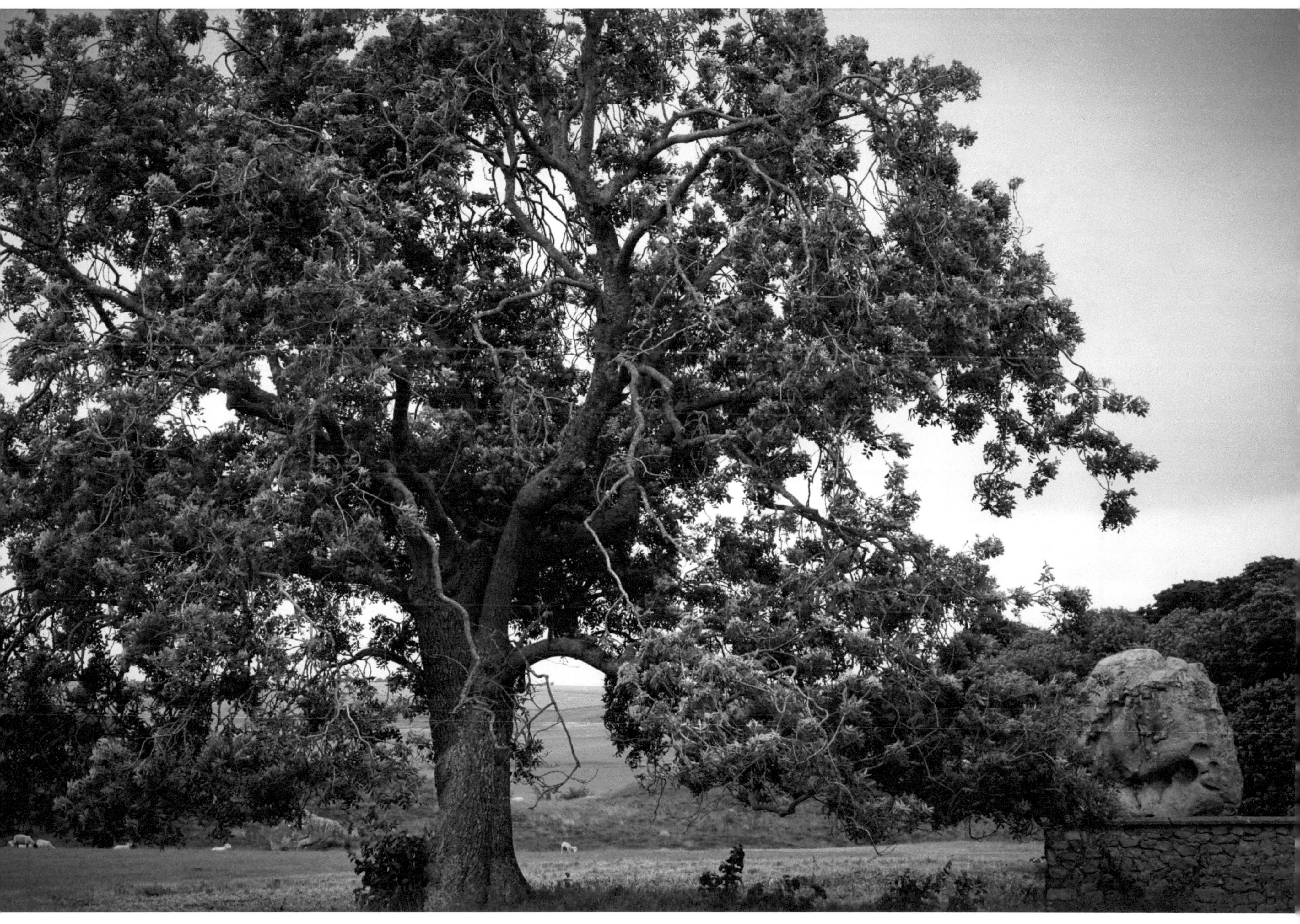

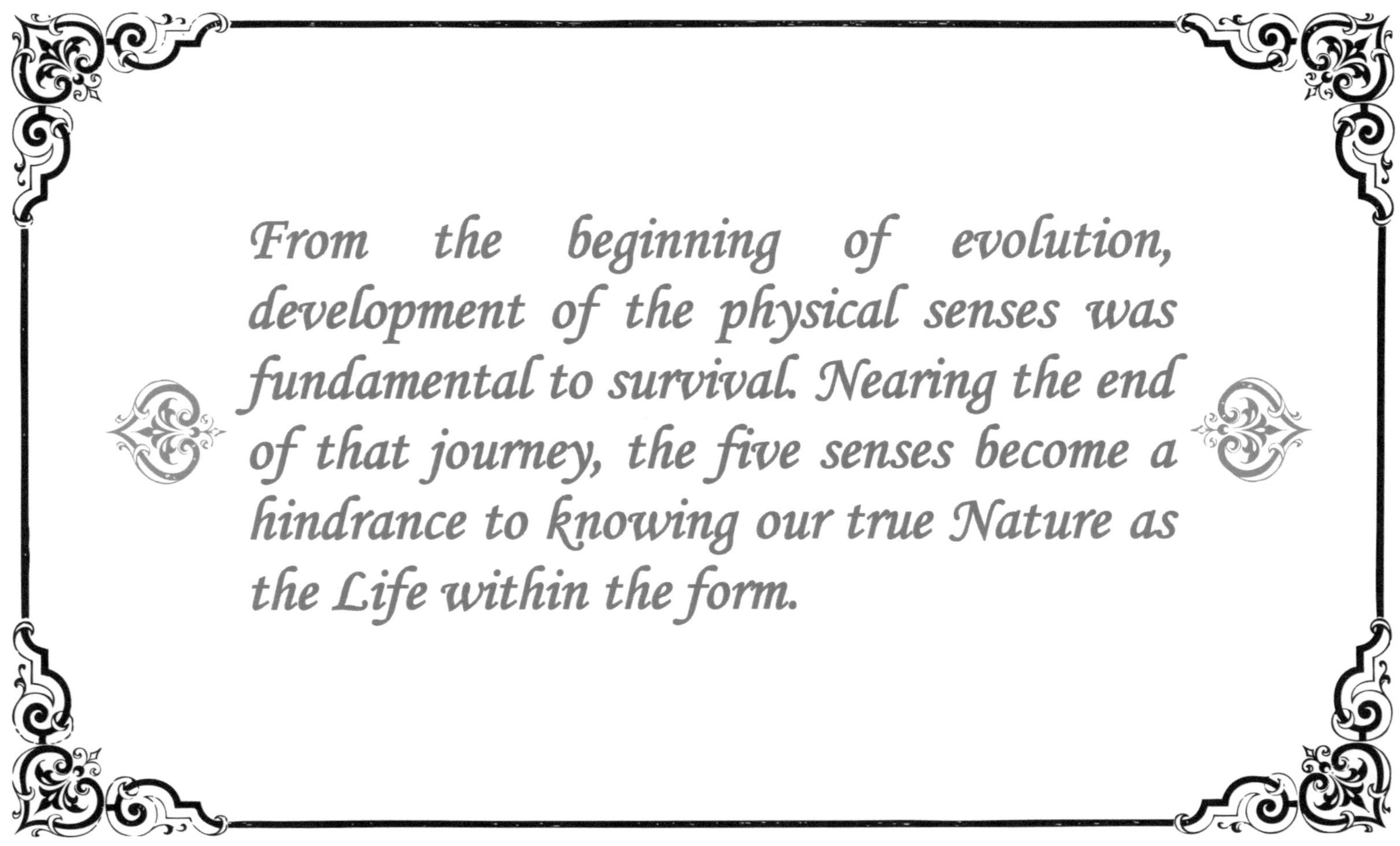

From the beginning of evolution, development of the physical senses was fundamental to survival. Nearing the end of that journey, the five senses become a hindrance to knowing our true Nature as the Life within the form.

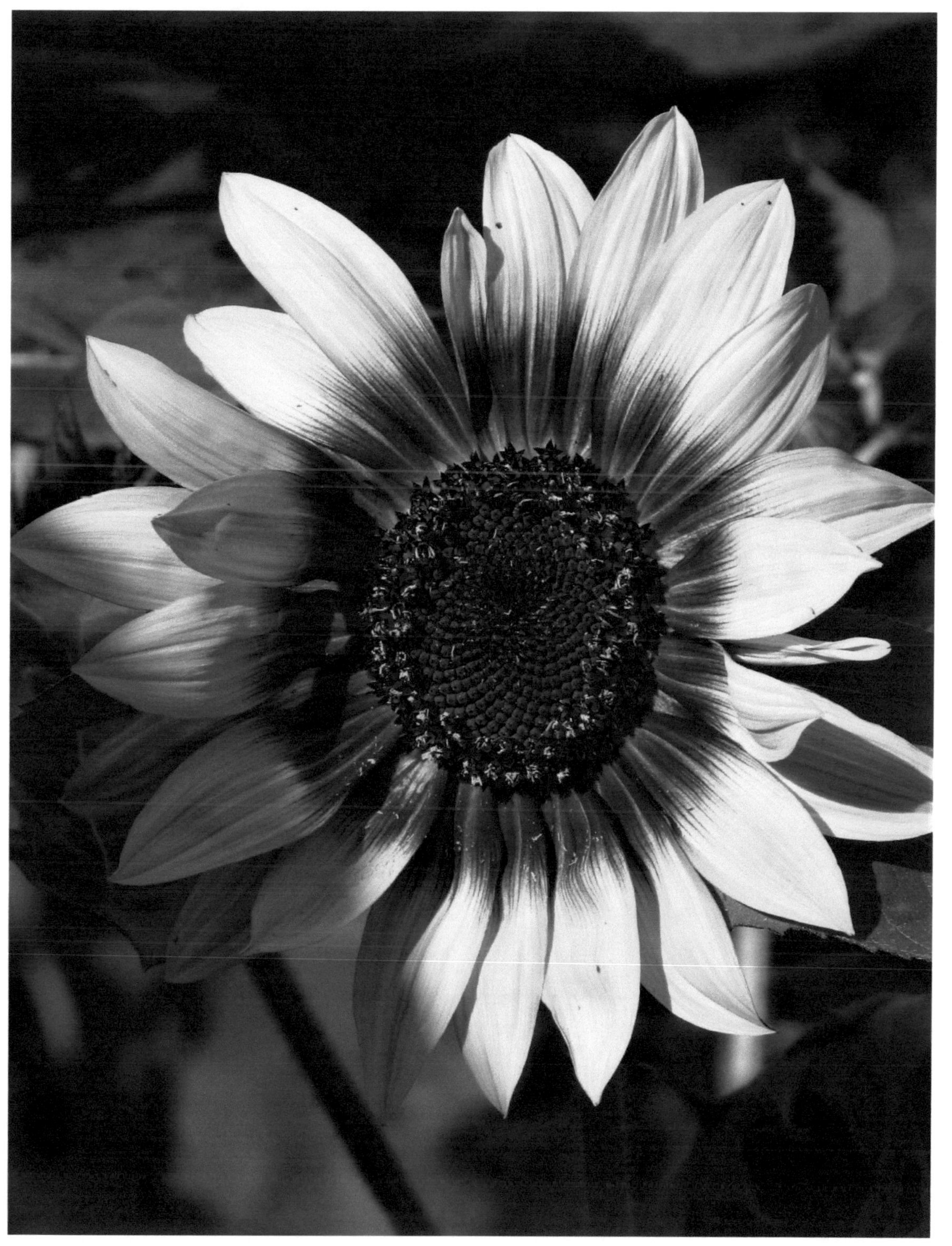

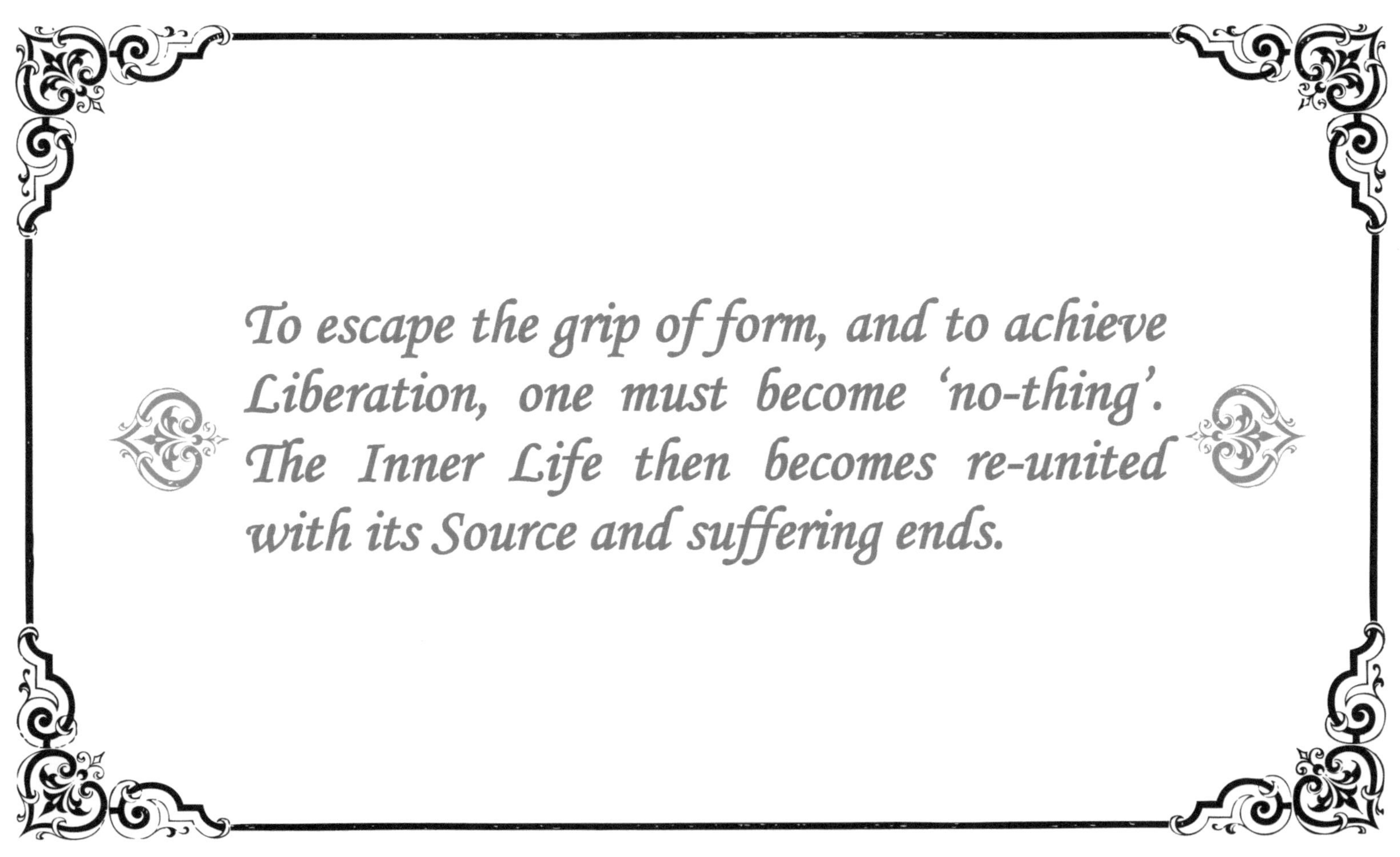

To escape the grip of form, and to achieve Liberation, one must become 'no-thing'. The Inner Life then becomes re-united with its Source and suffering ends.

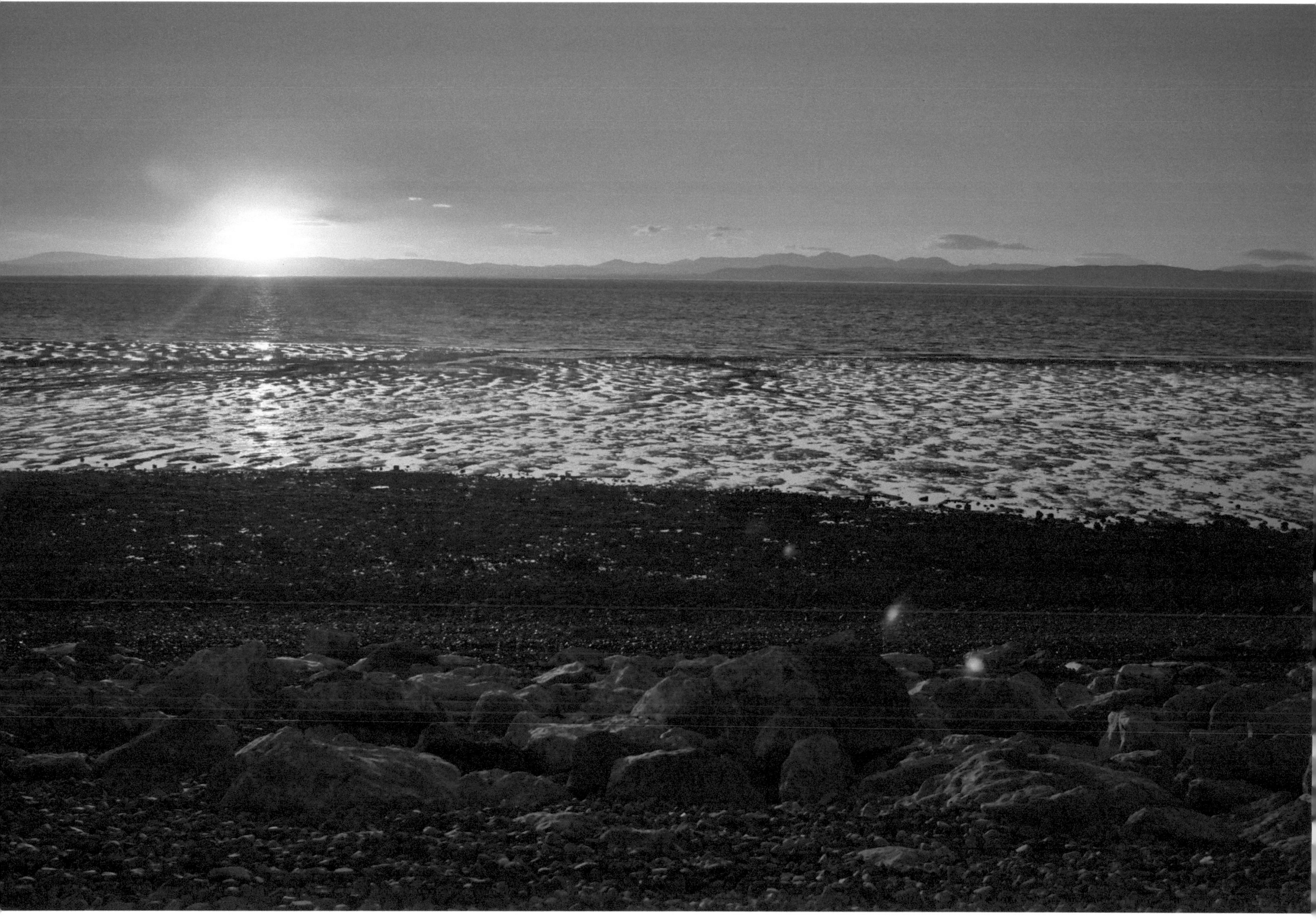

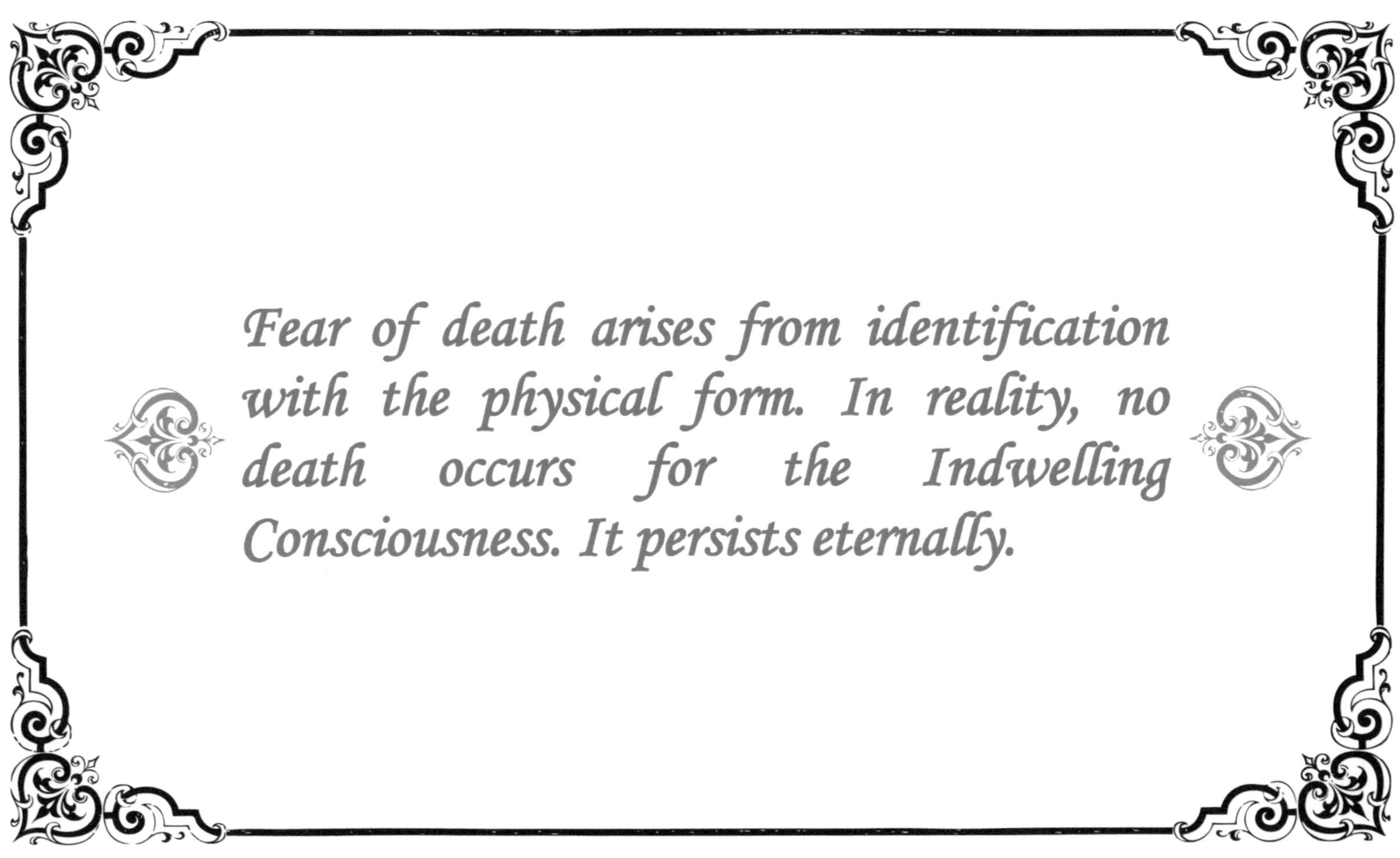

Fear of death arises from identification with the physical form. In reality, no death occurs for the Indwelling Consciousness. It persists eternally.

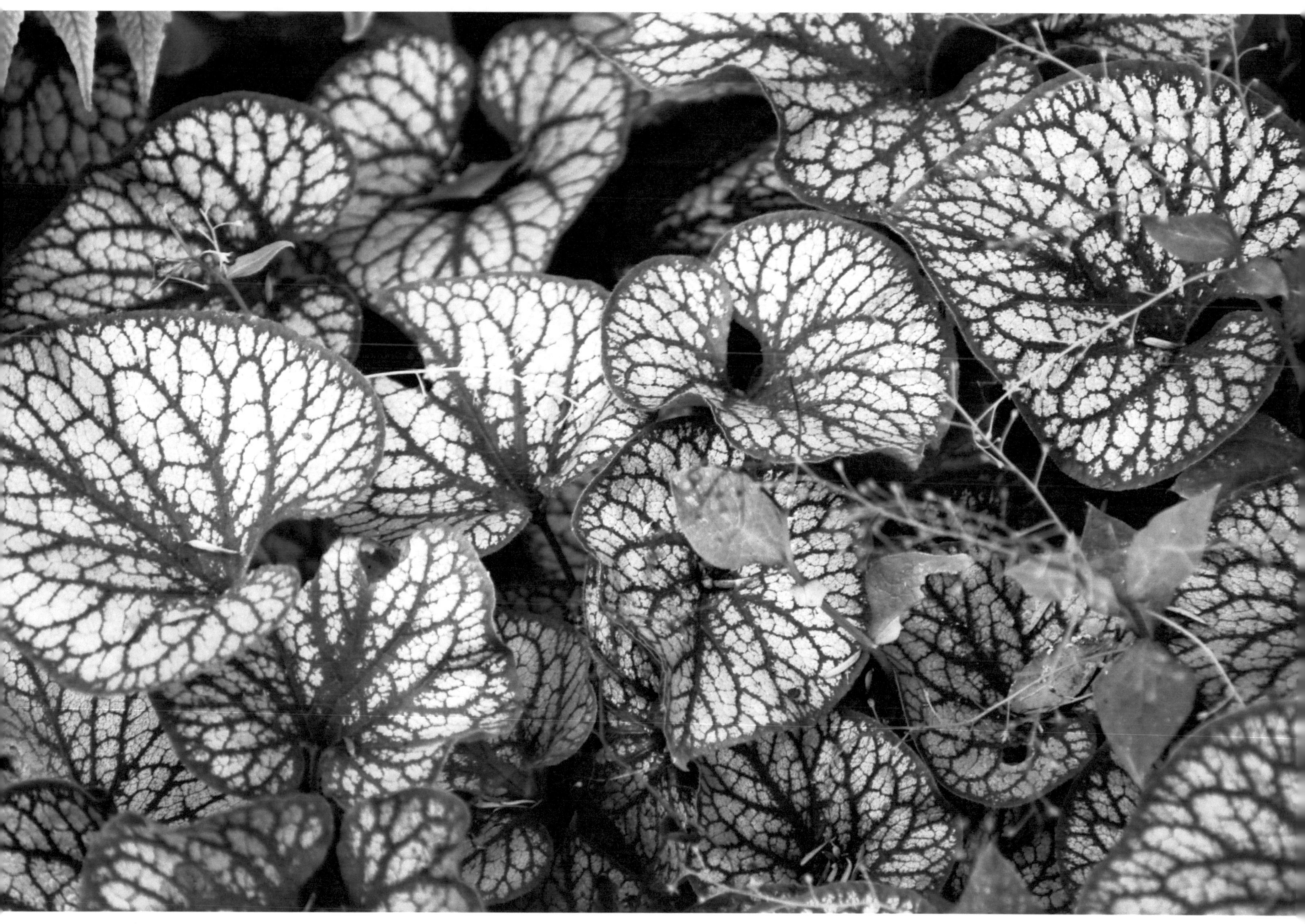

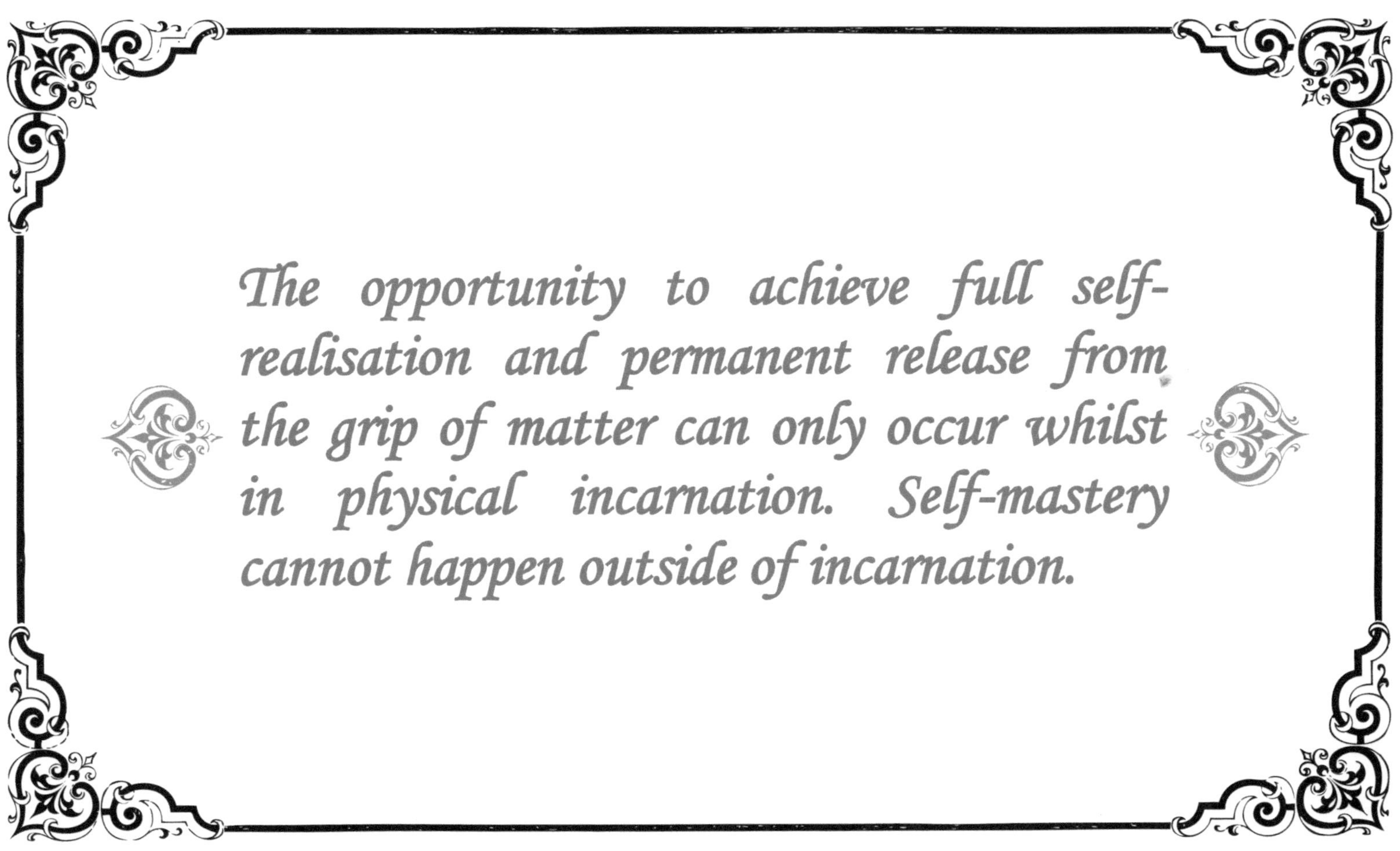

The opportunity to achieve full self-realisation and permanent release from the grip of matter can only occur whilst in physical incarnation. Self-mastery cannot happen outside of incarnation.

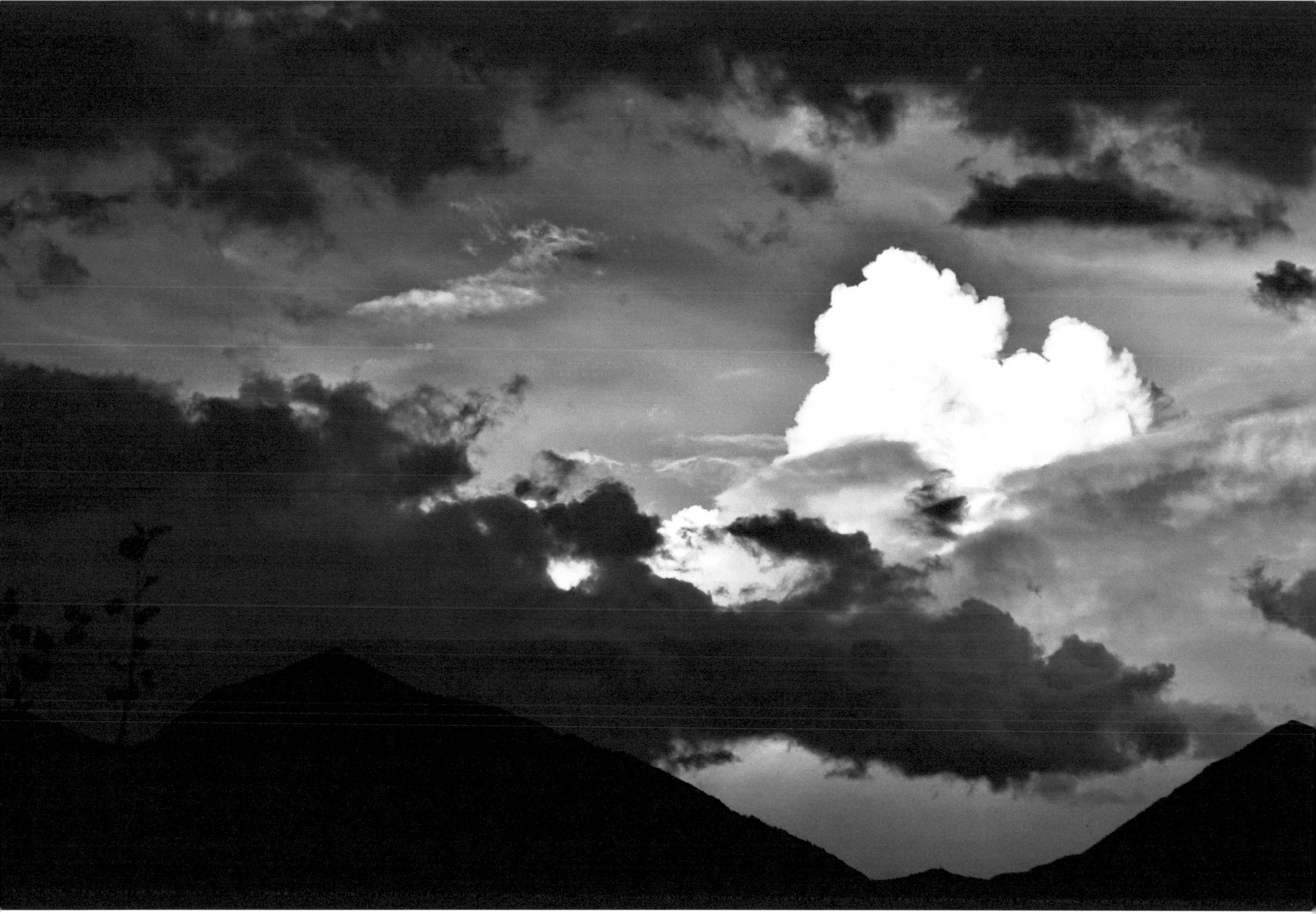

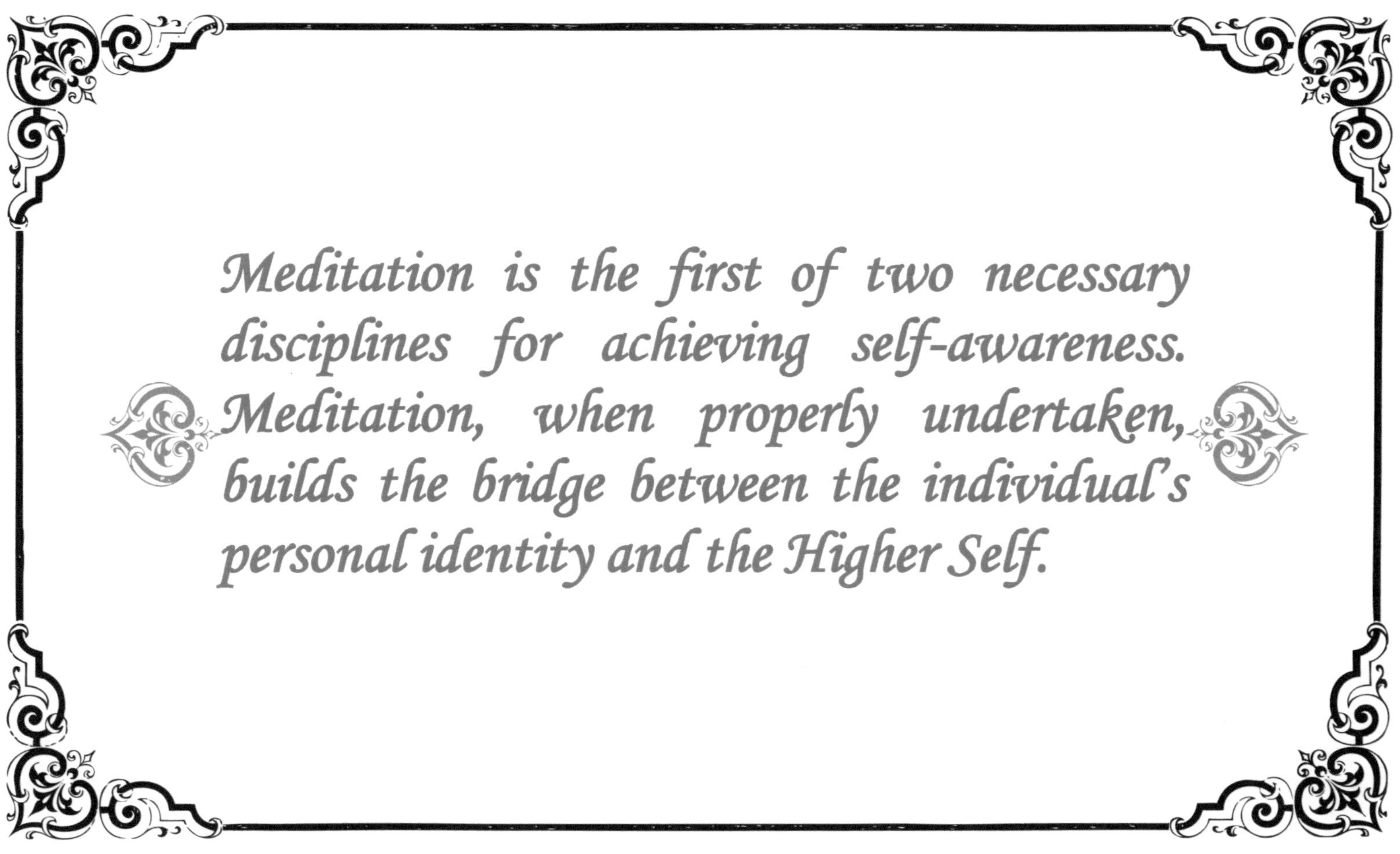

Meditation is the first of two necessary disciplines for achieving self-awareness. Meditation, when properly undertaken, builds the bridge between the individual's personal identity and the Higher Self.

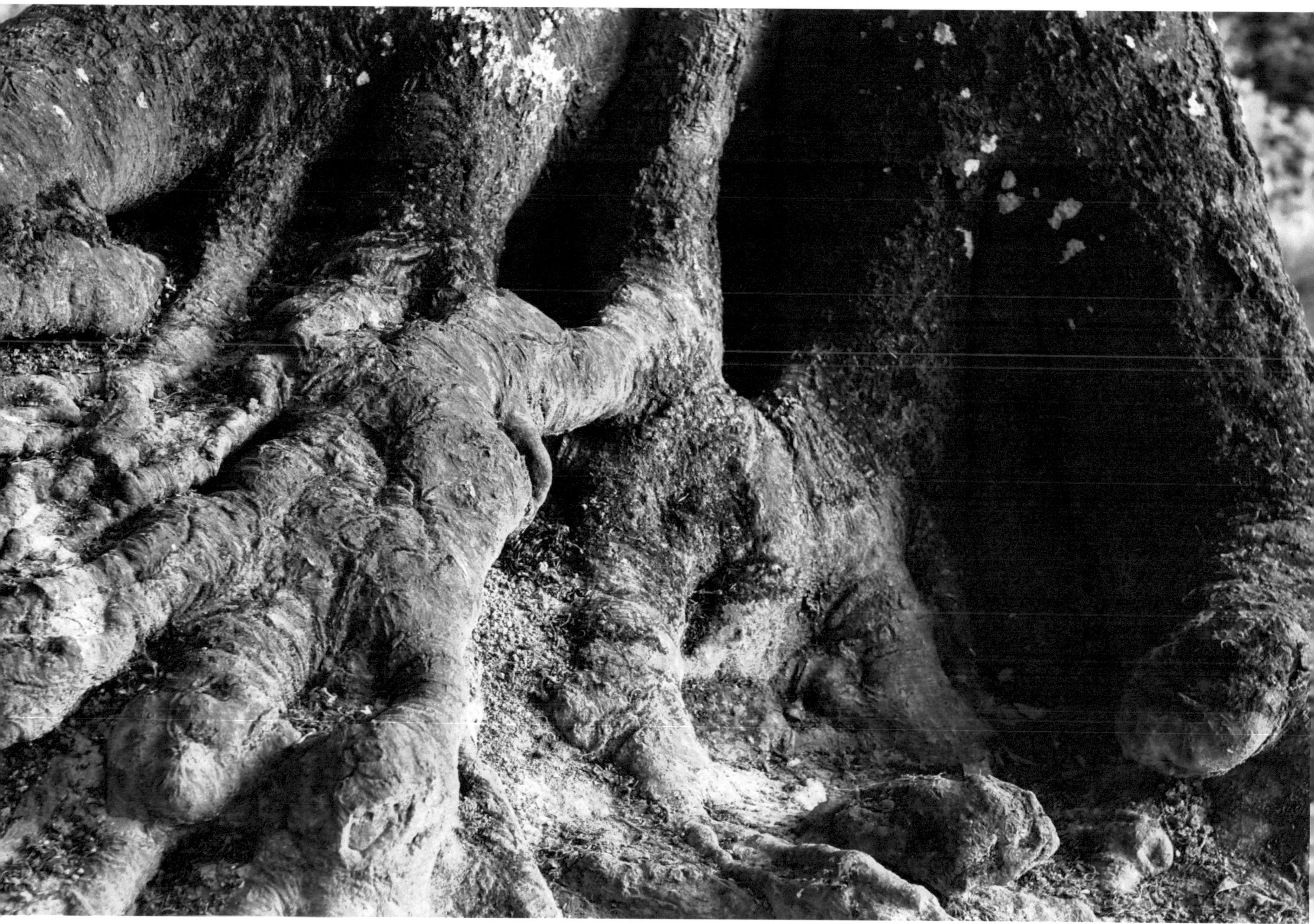

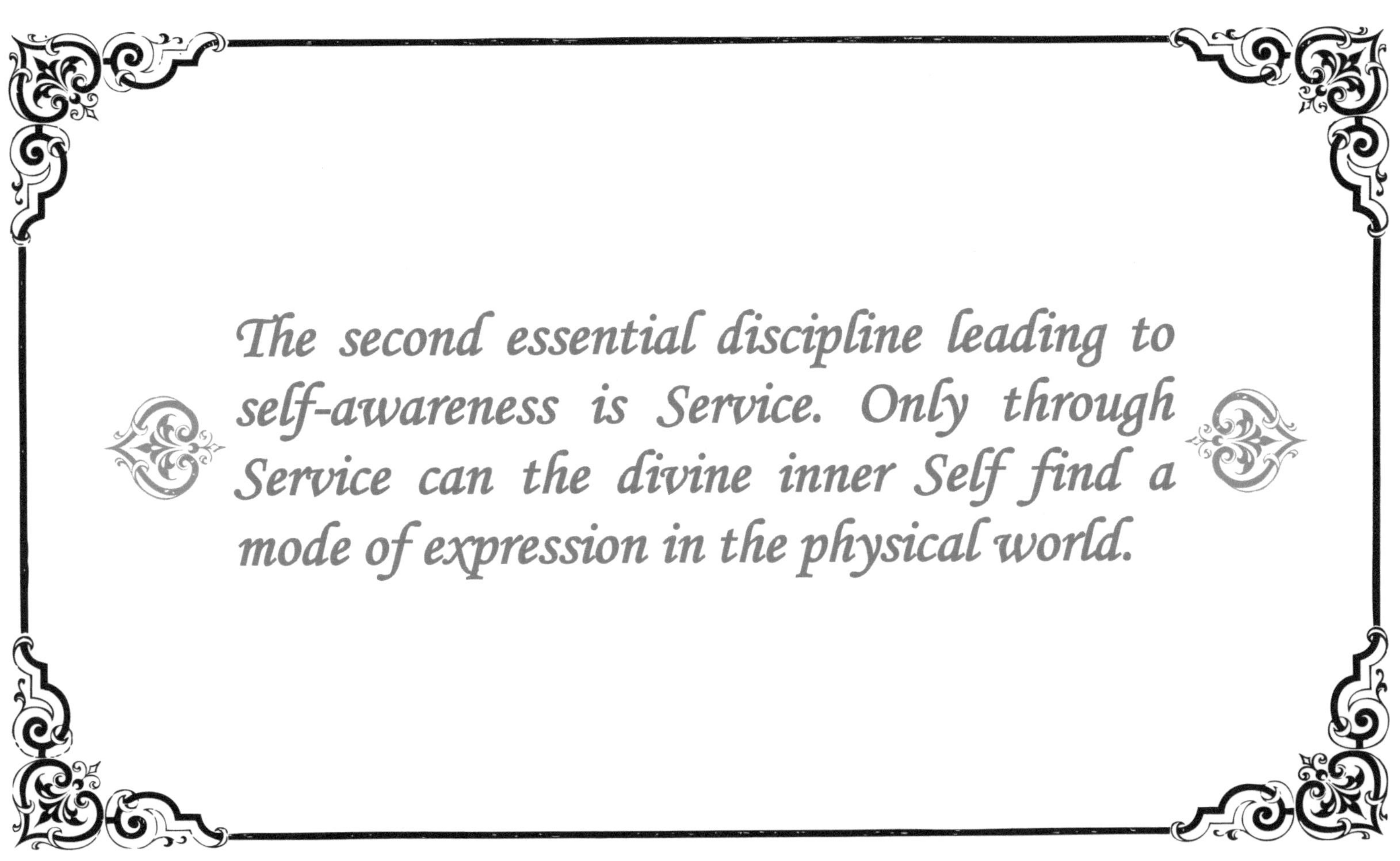

The second essential discipline leading to self-awareness is Service. Only through Service can the divine inner Self find a mode of expression in the physical world.

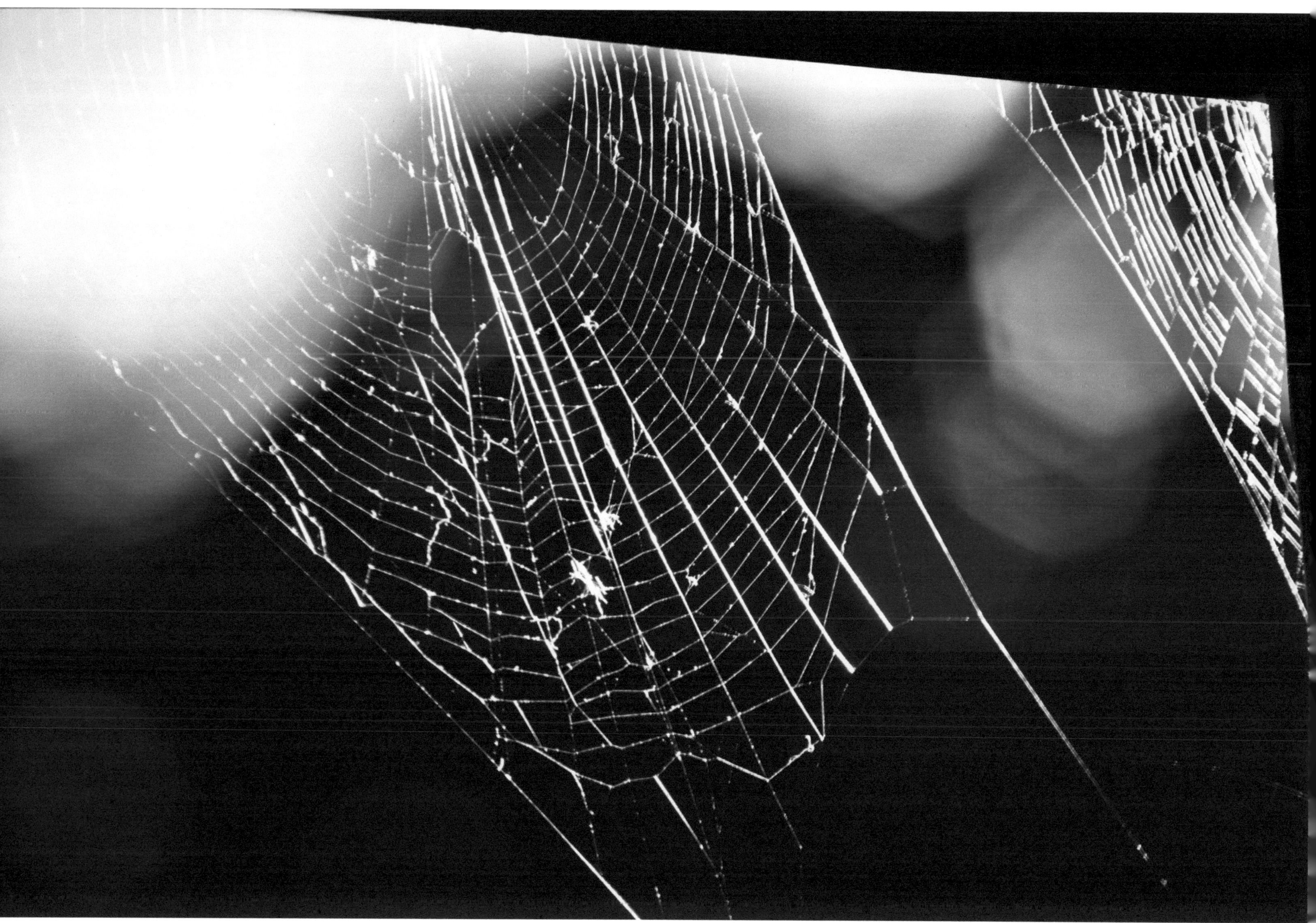

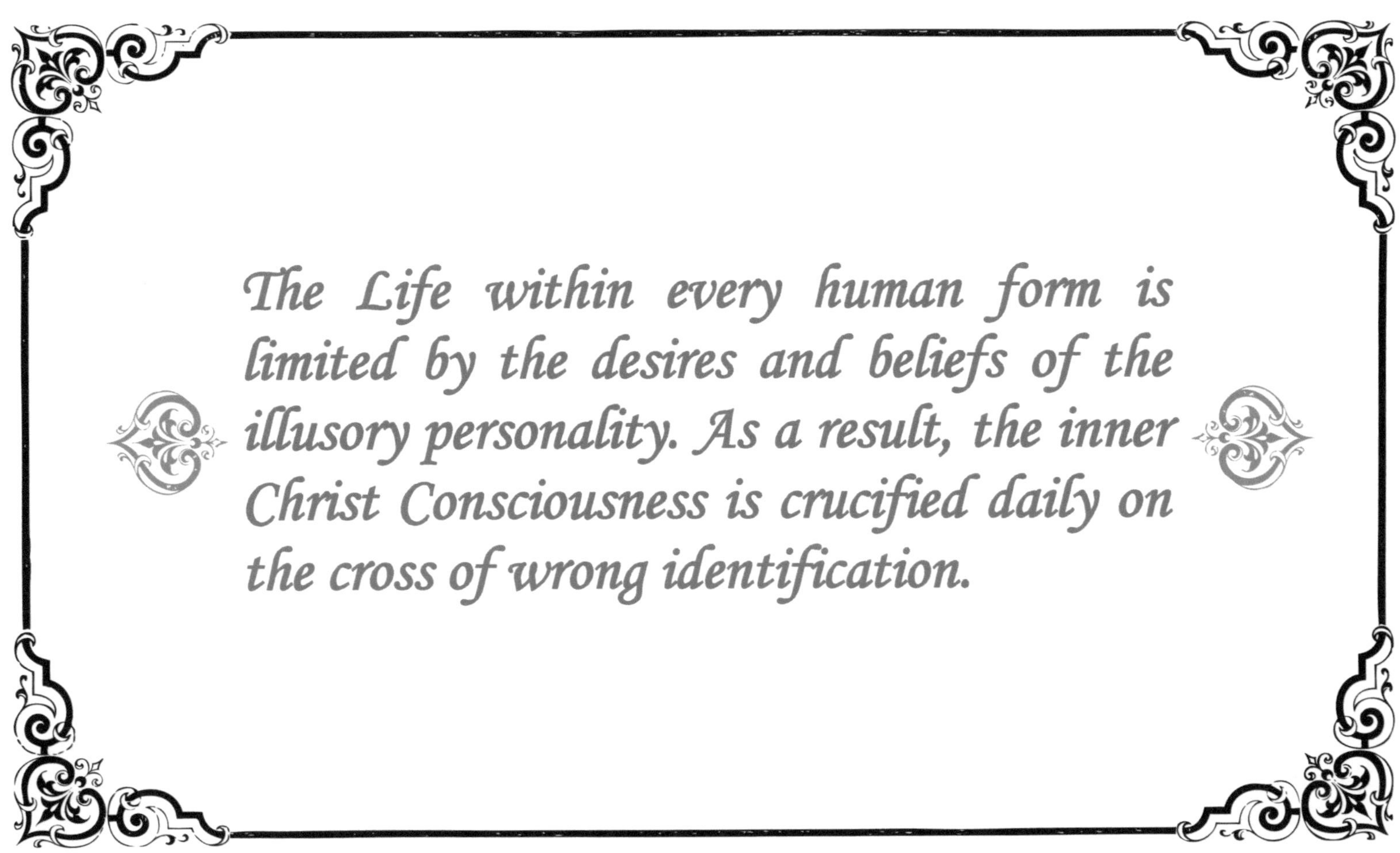

The Life within every human form is limited by the desires and beliefs of the illusory personality. As a result, the inner Christ Consciousness is crucified daily on the cross of wrong identification.

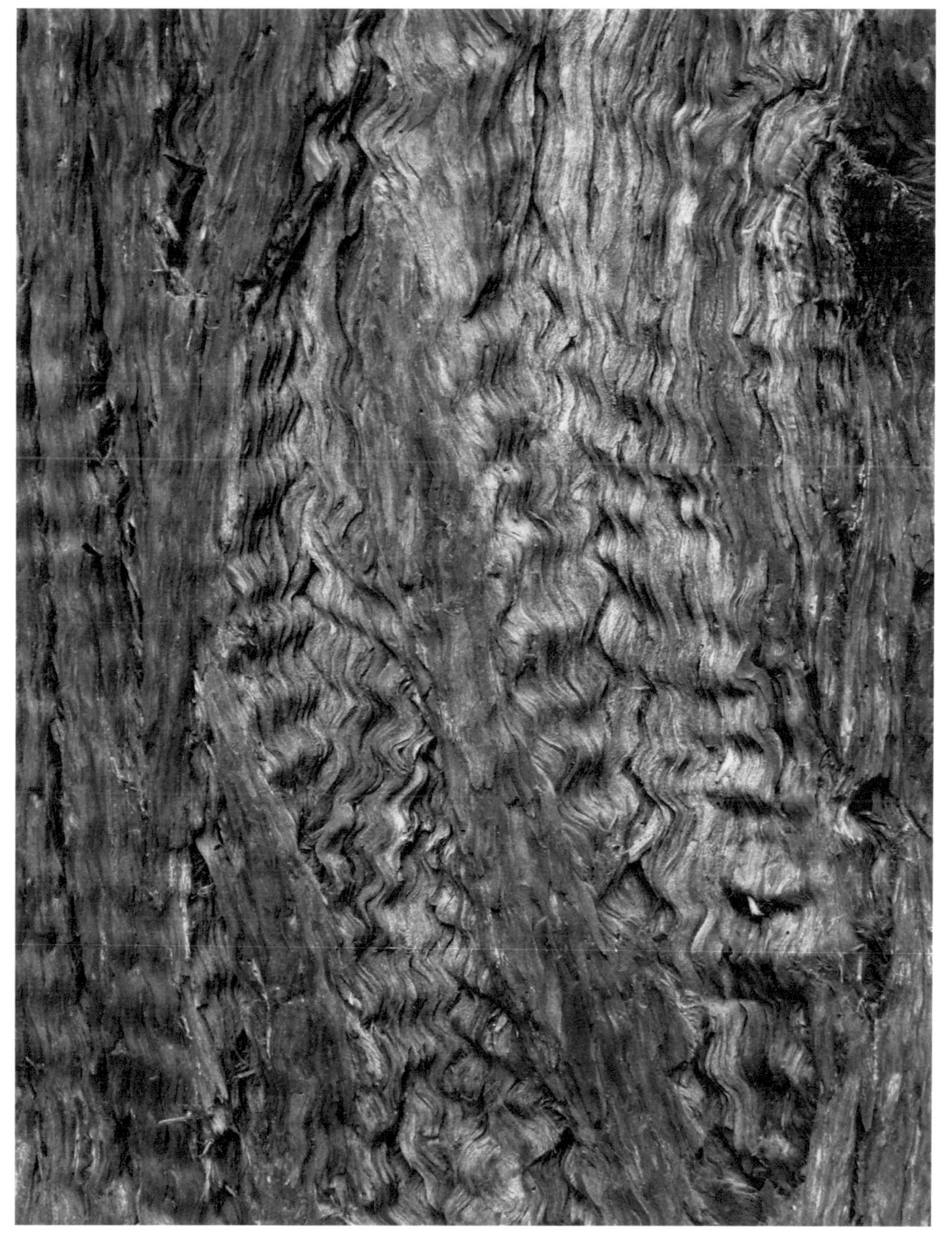

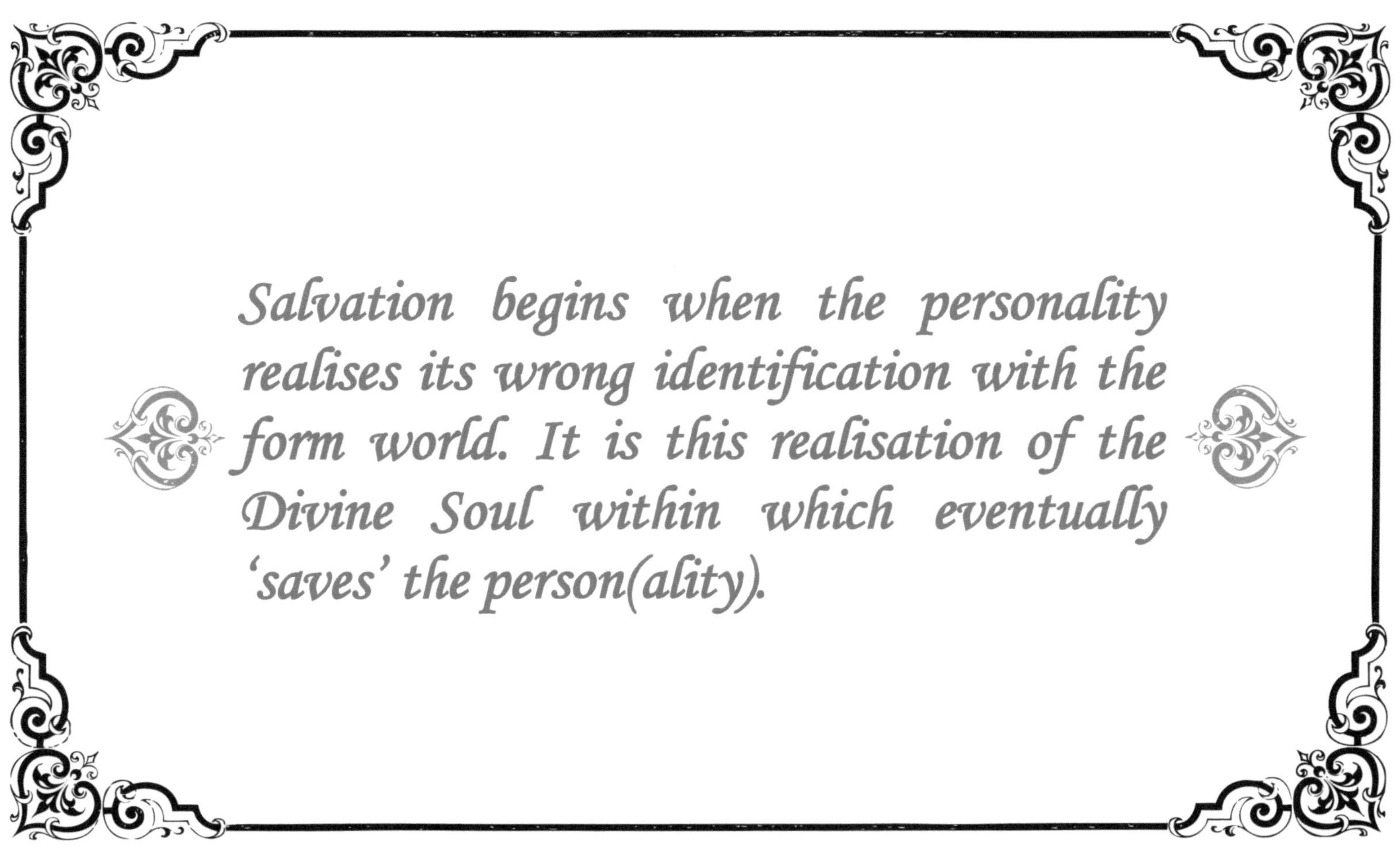

Salvation begins when the personality realises its wrong identification with the form world. It is this realisation of the Divine Soul within which eventually 'saves' the person(ality).

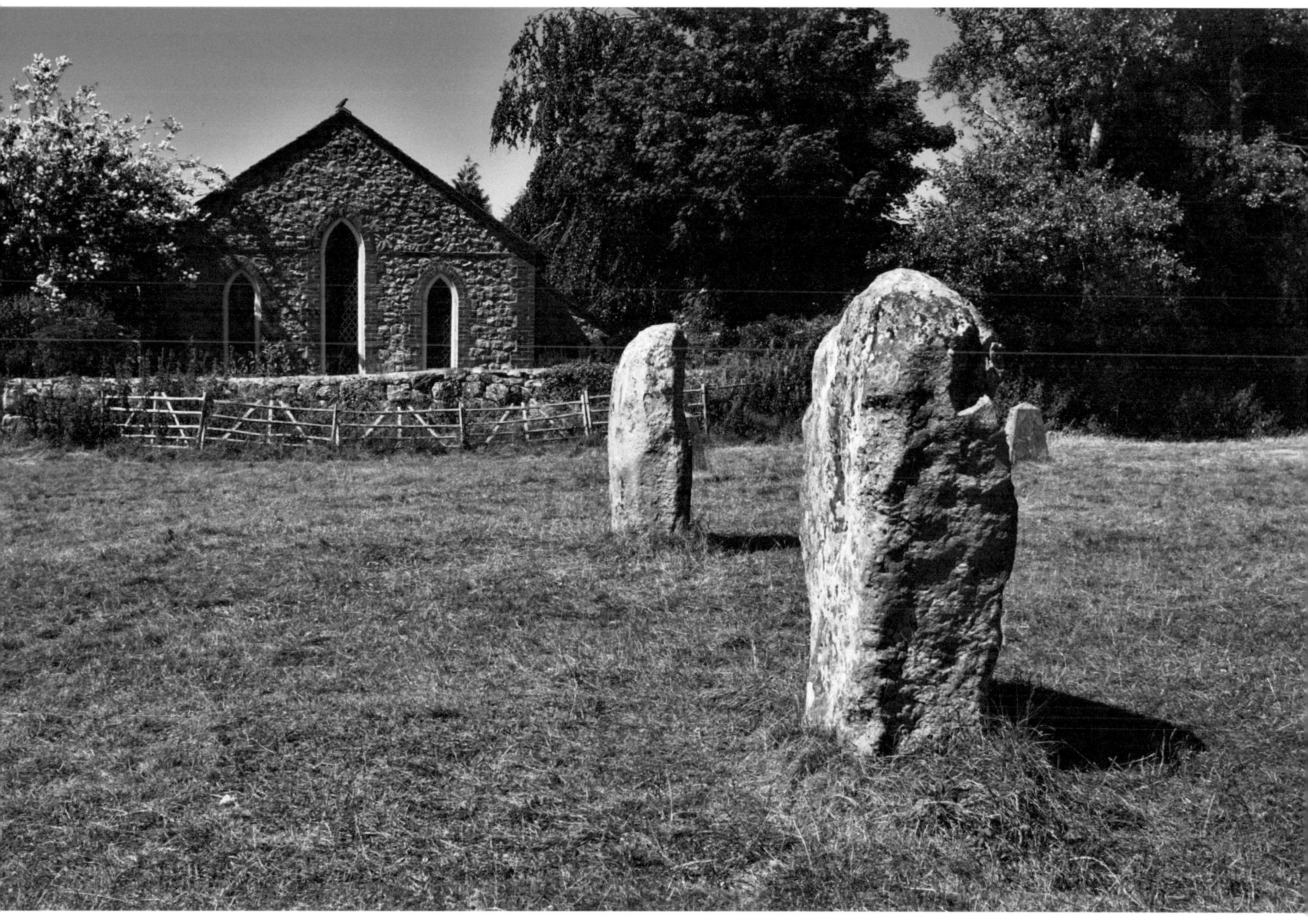

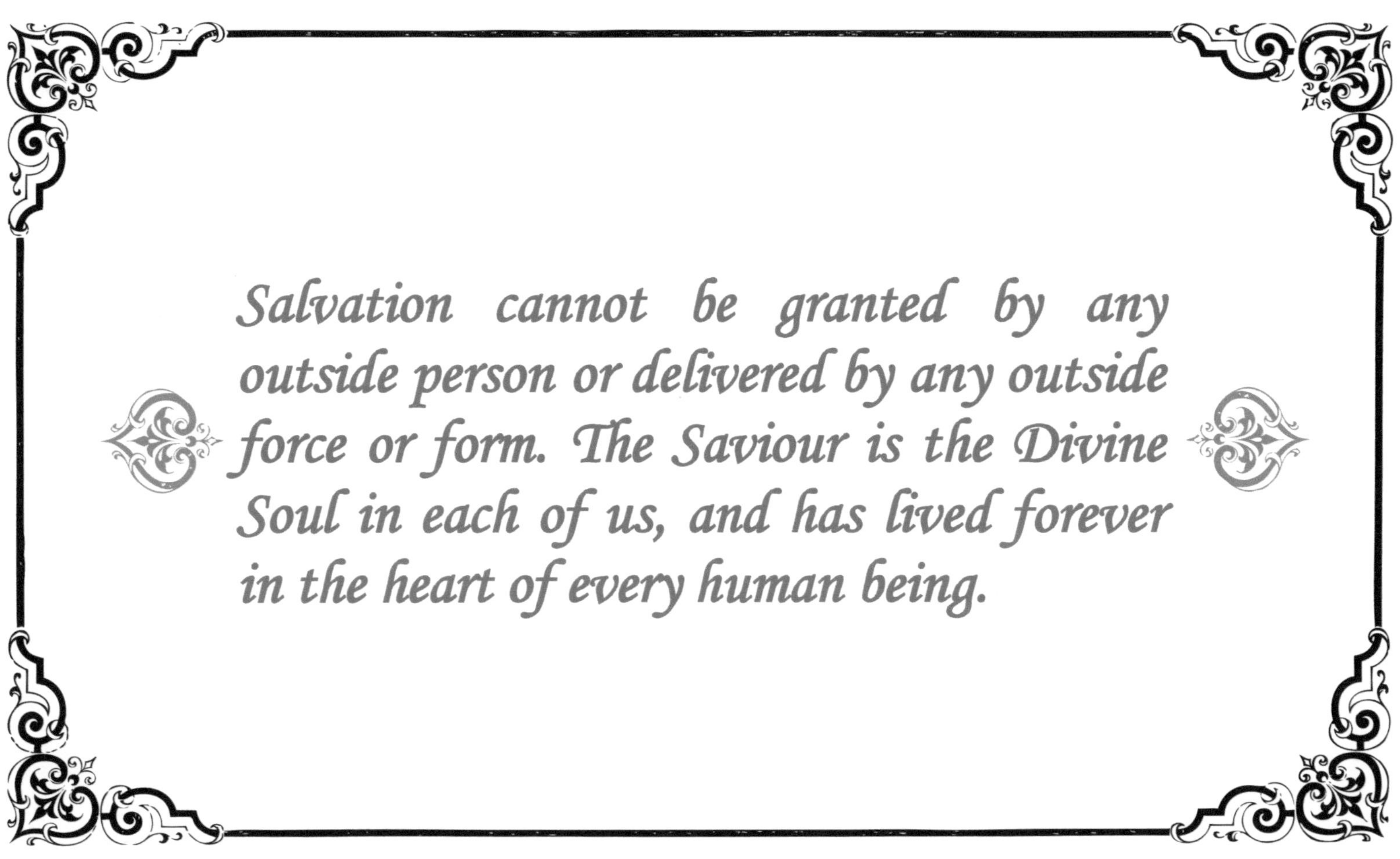

Salvation cannot be granted by any outside person or delivered by any outside force or form. The Saviour is the Divine Soul in each of us, and has lived forever in the heart of every human being.

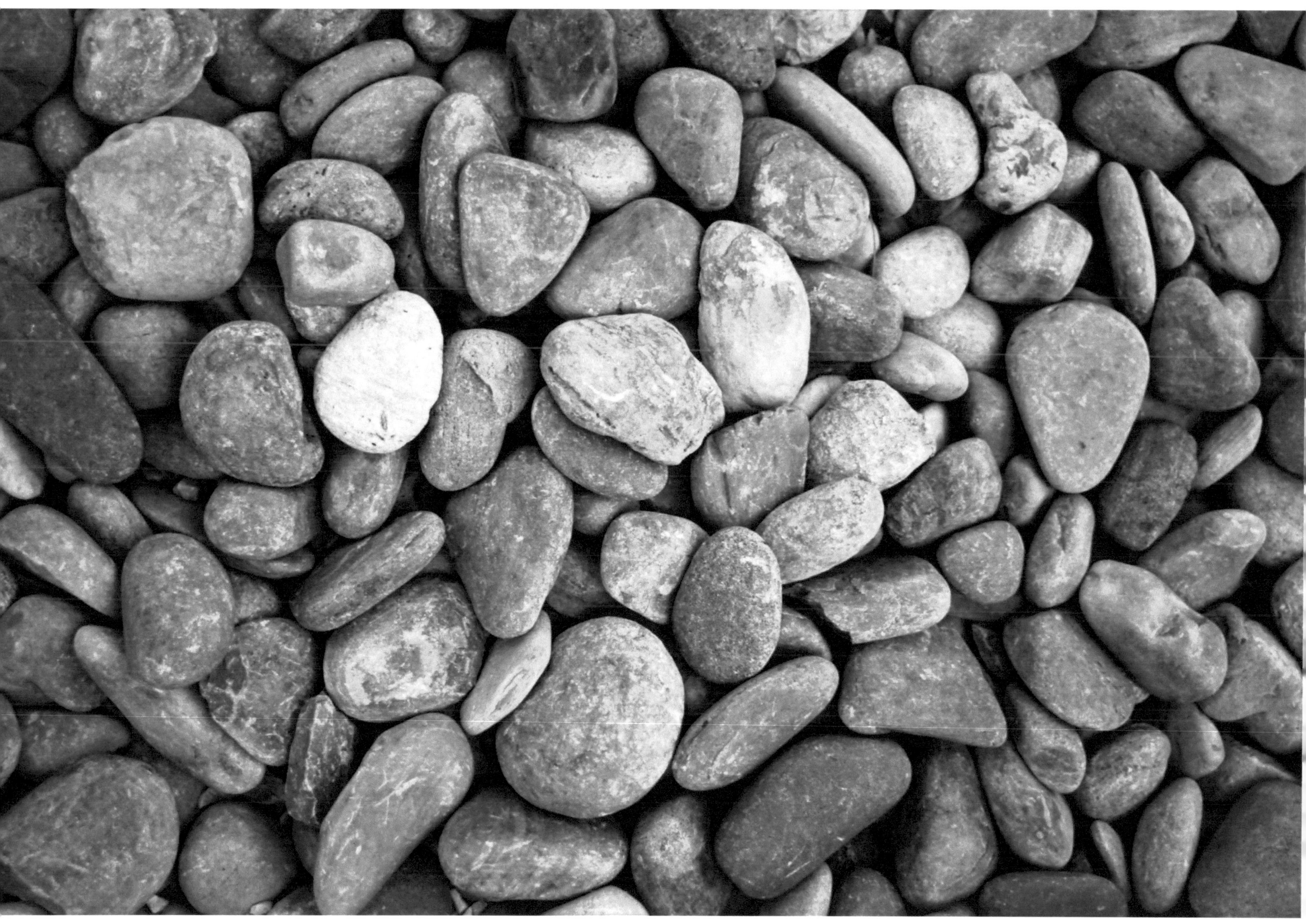

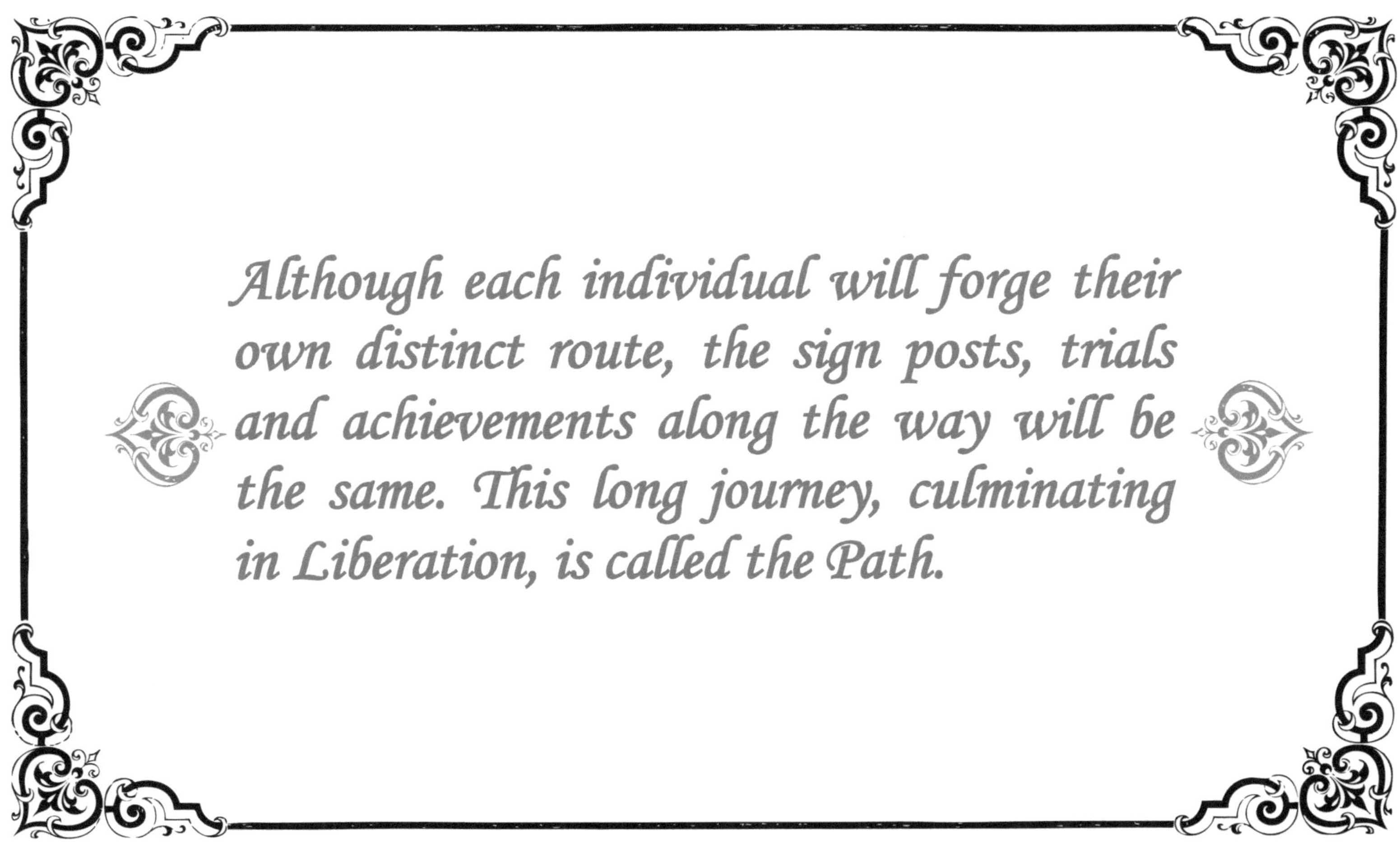

Although each individual will forge their own distinct route, the sign posts, trials and achievements along the way will be the same. This long journey, culminating in Liberation, is called the Path.

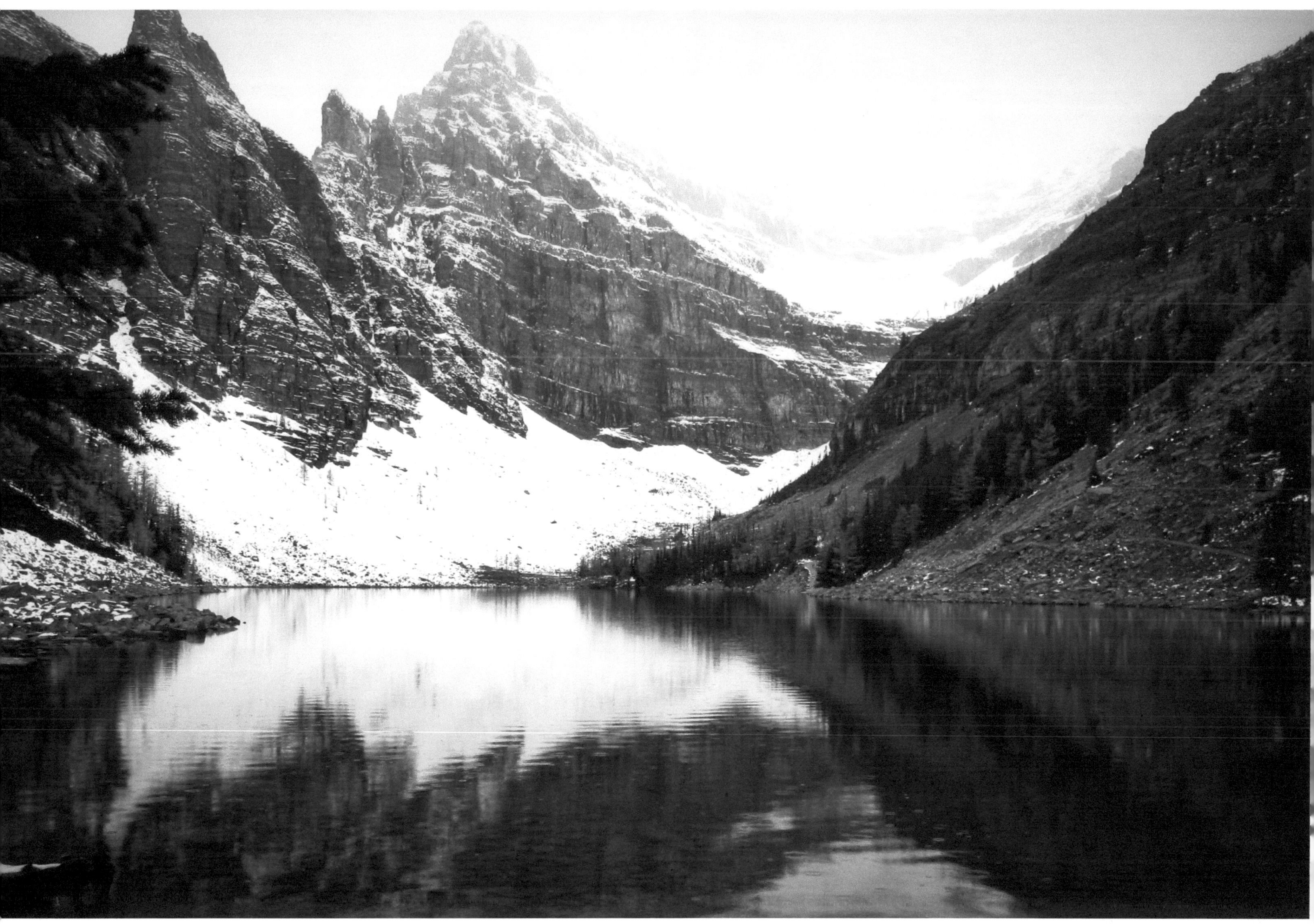

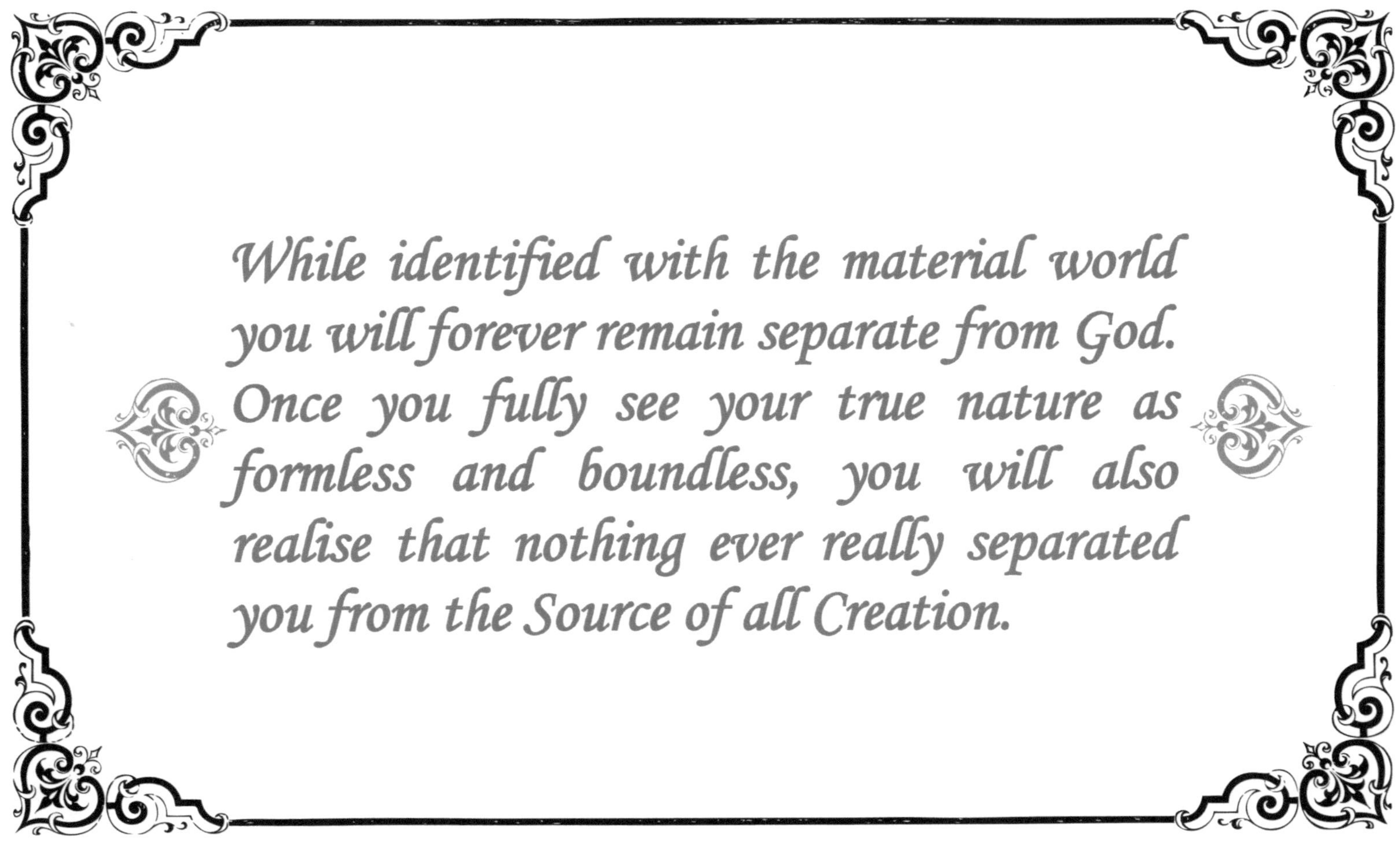

While identified with the material world you will forever remain separate from God. Once you fully see your true nature as formless and boundless, you will also realise that nothing ever really separated you from the Source of all Creation.

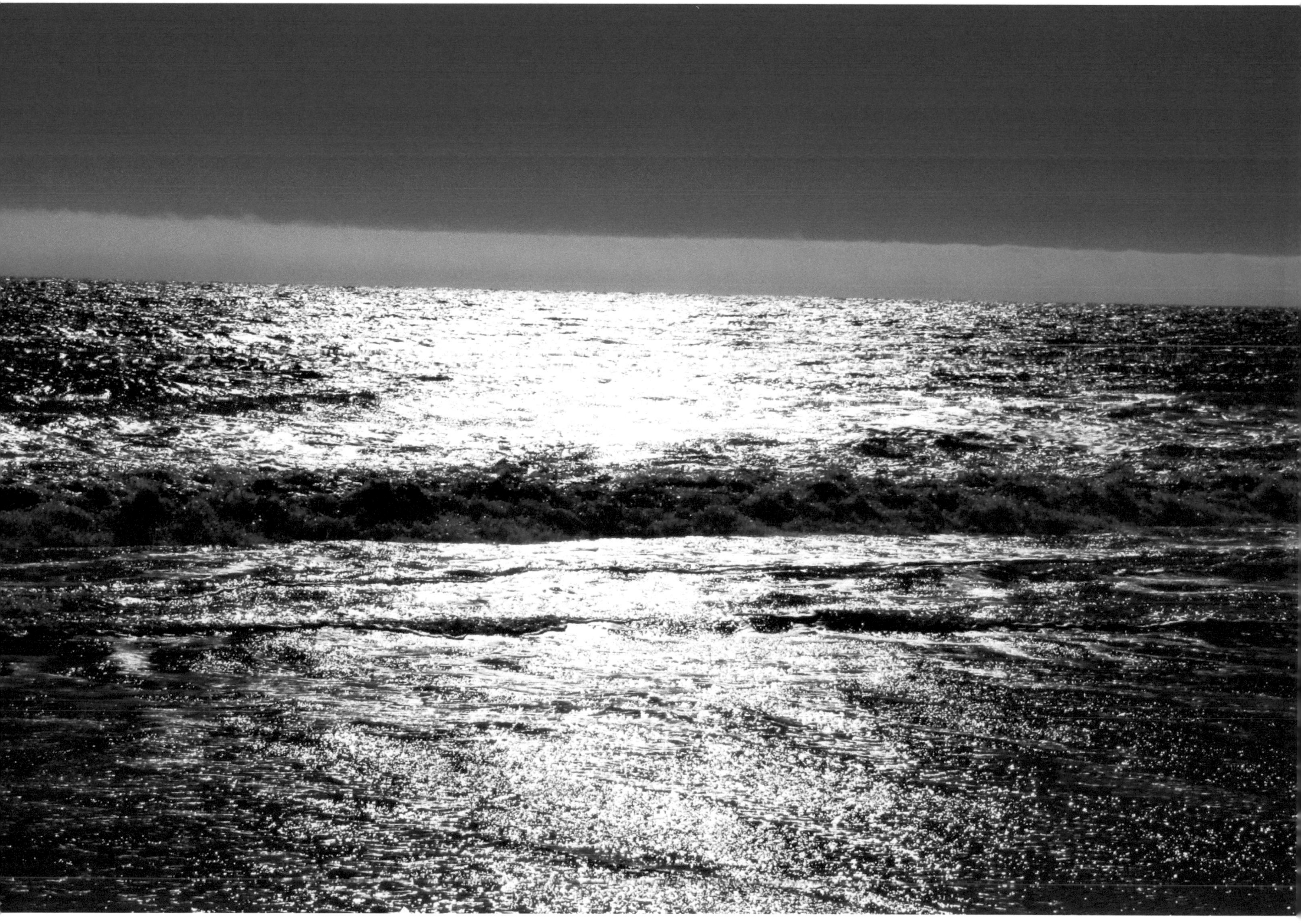

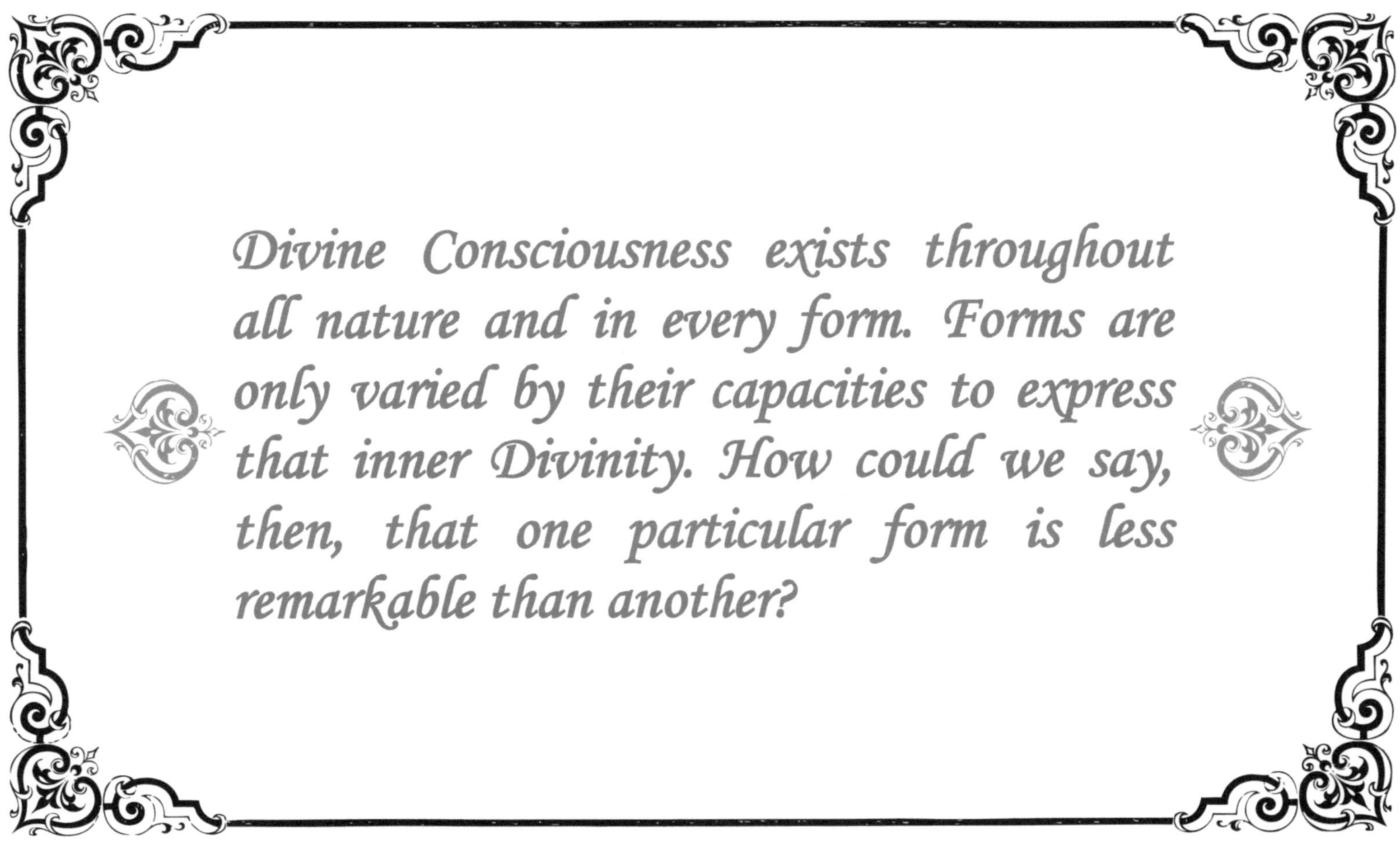

Divine Consciousness exists throughout all nature and in every form. Forms are only varied by their capacities to express that inner Divinity. How could we say, then, that one particular form is less remarkable than another?

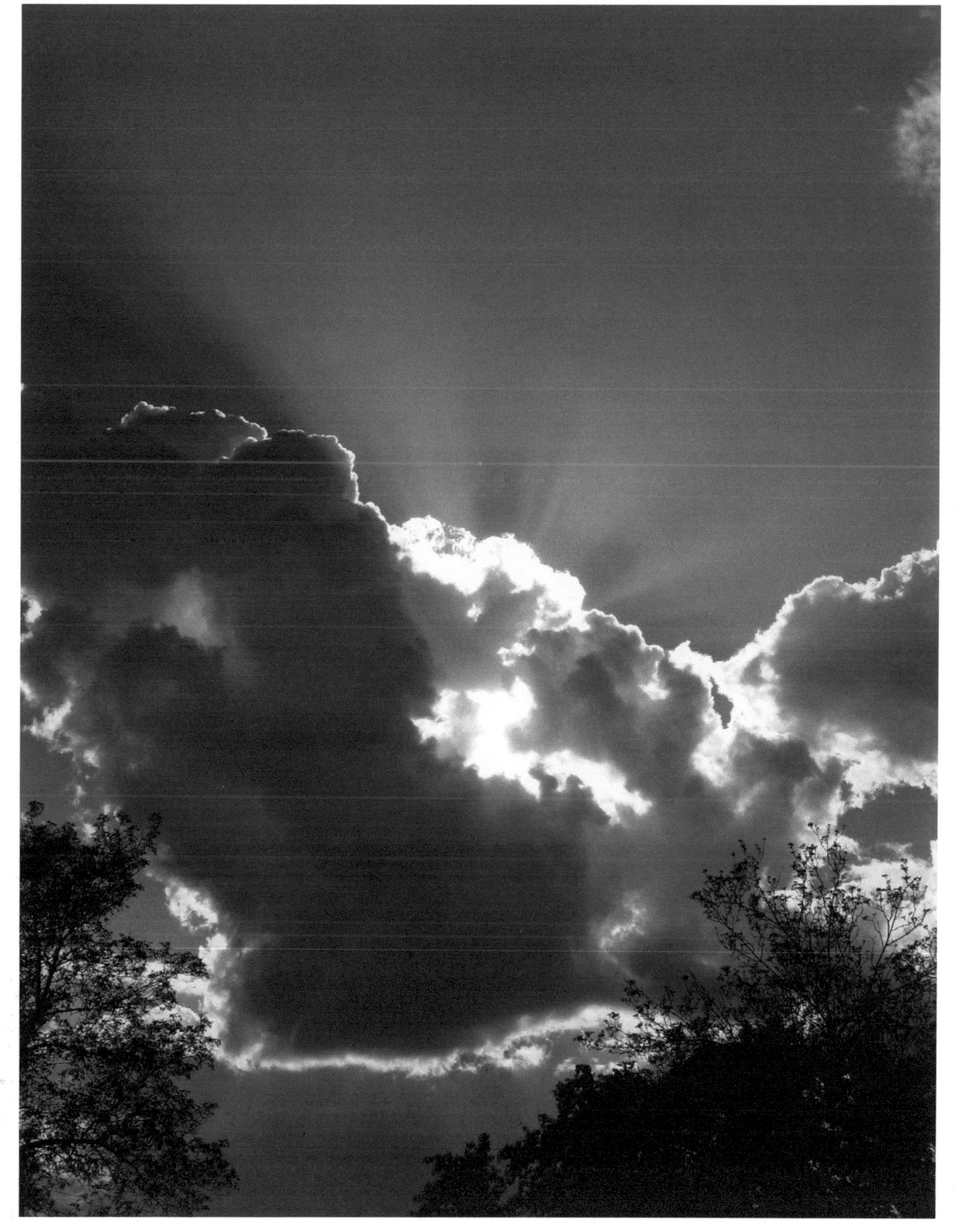

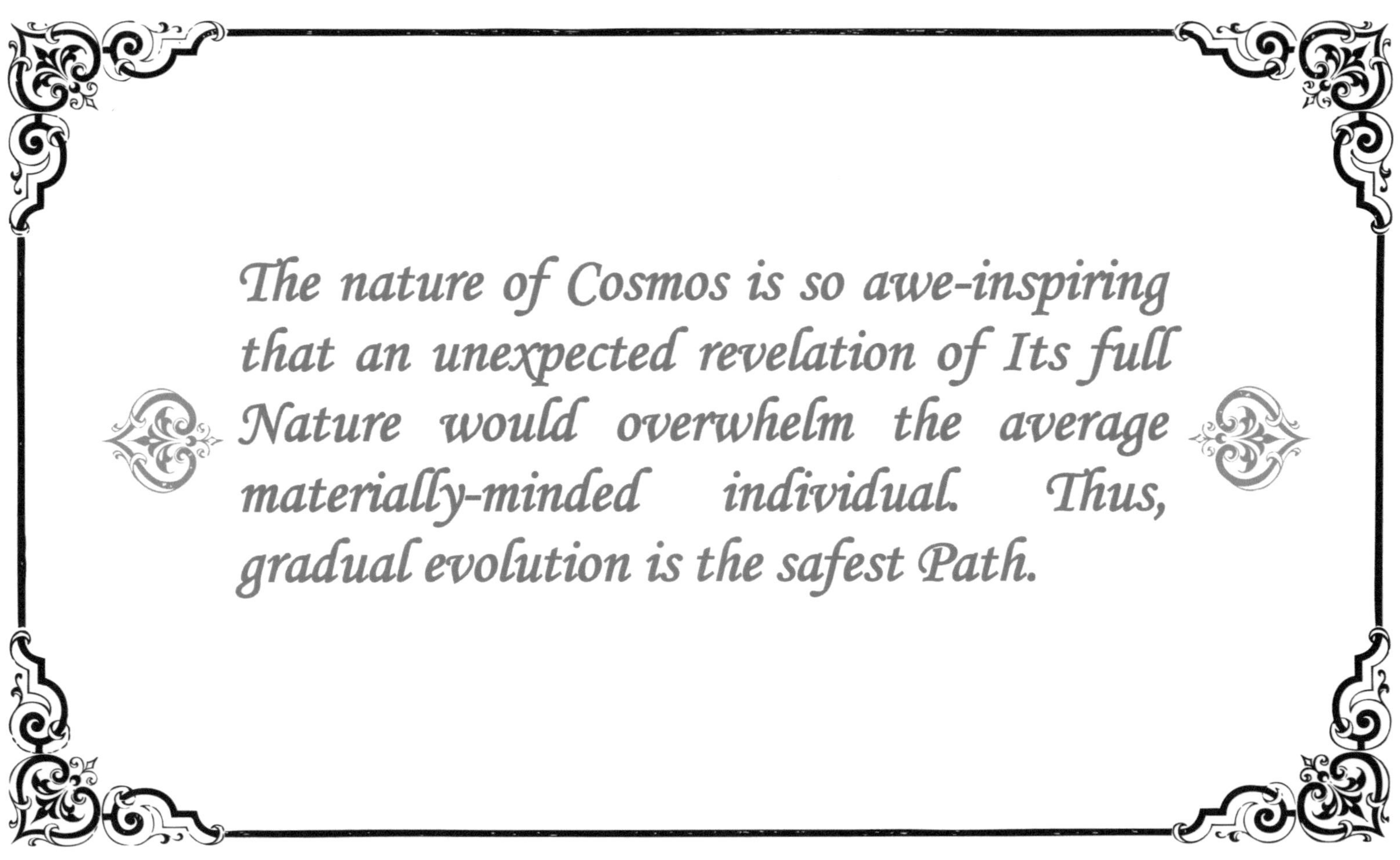

The nature of Cosmos is so awe-inspiring that an unexpected revelation of Its full Nature would overwhelm the average materially-minded individual. Thus, gradual evolution is the safest Path.

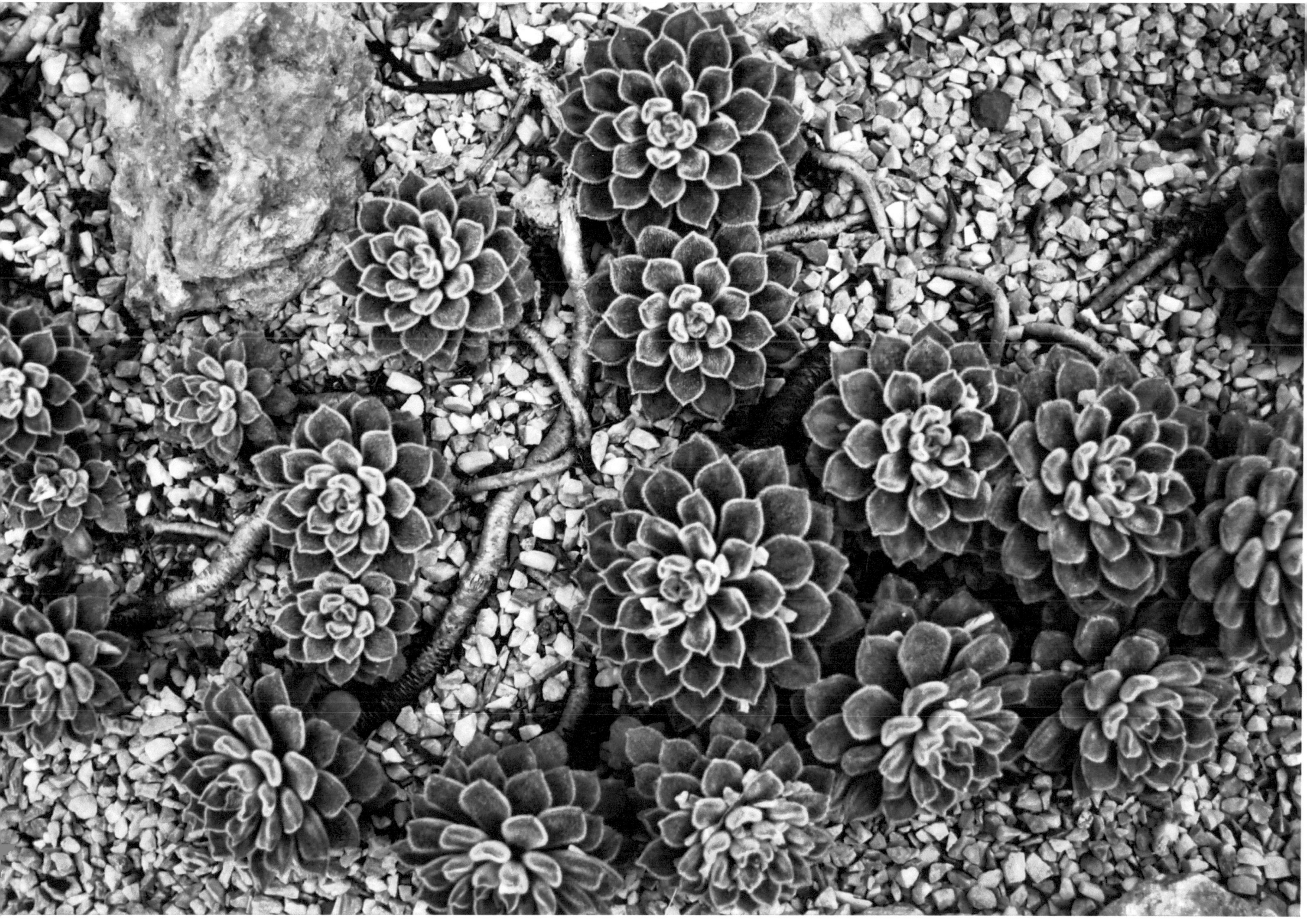

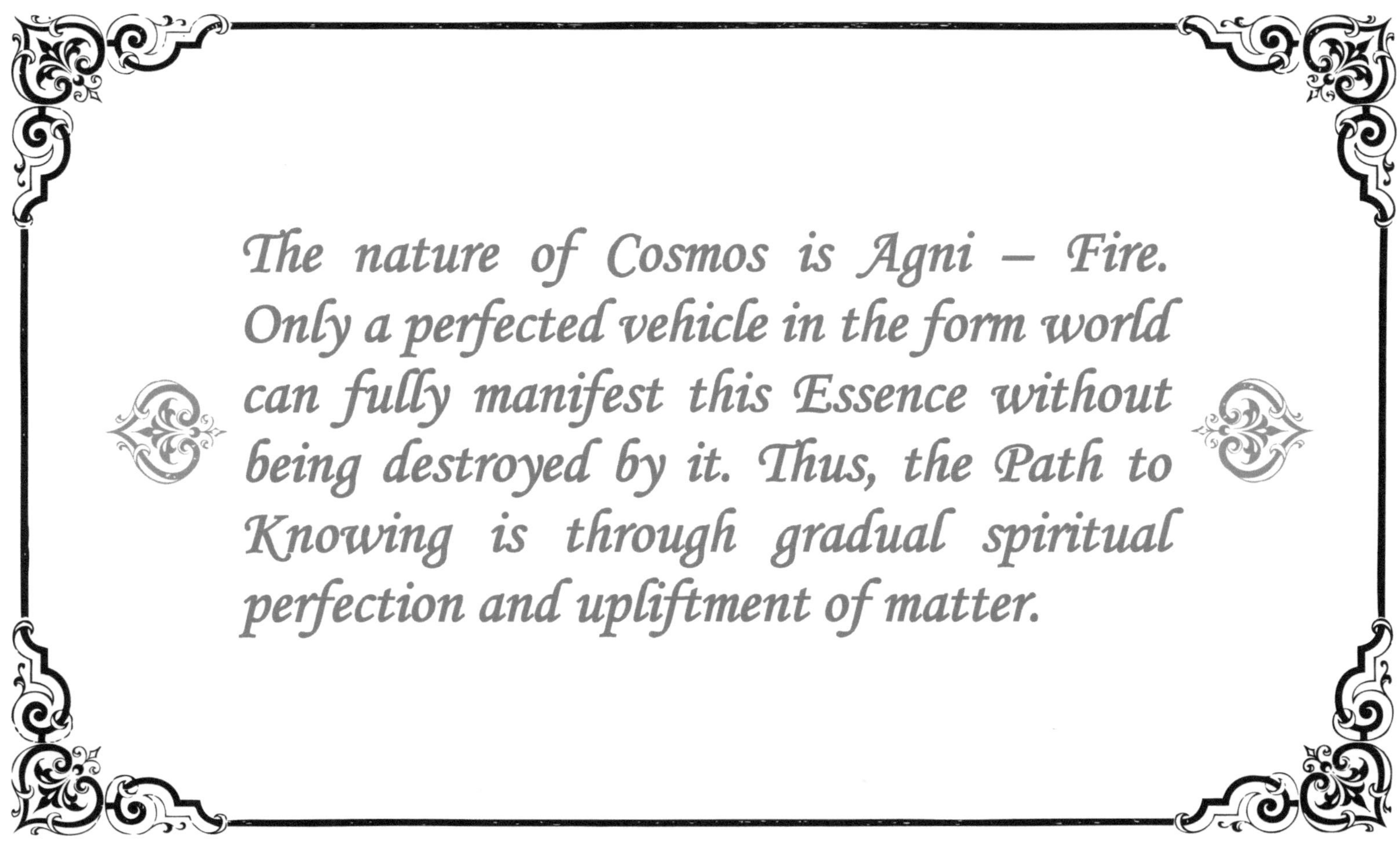

The nature of Cosmos is Agni – Fire. Only a perfected vehicle in the form world can fully manifest this Essence without being destroyed by it. Thus, the Path to Knowing is through gradual spiritual perfection and upliftment of matter.

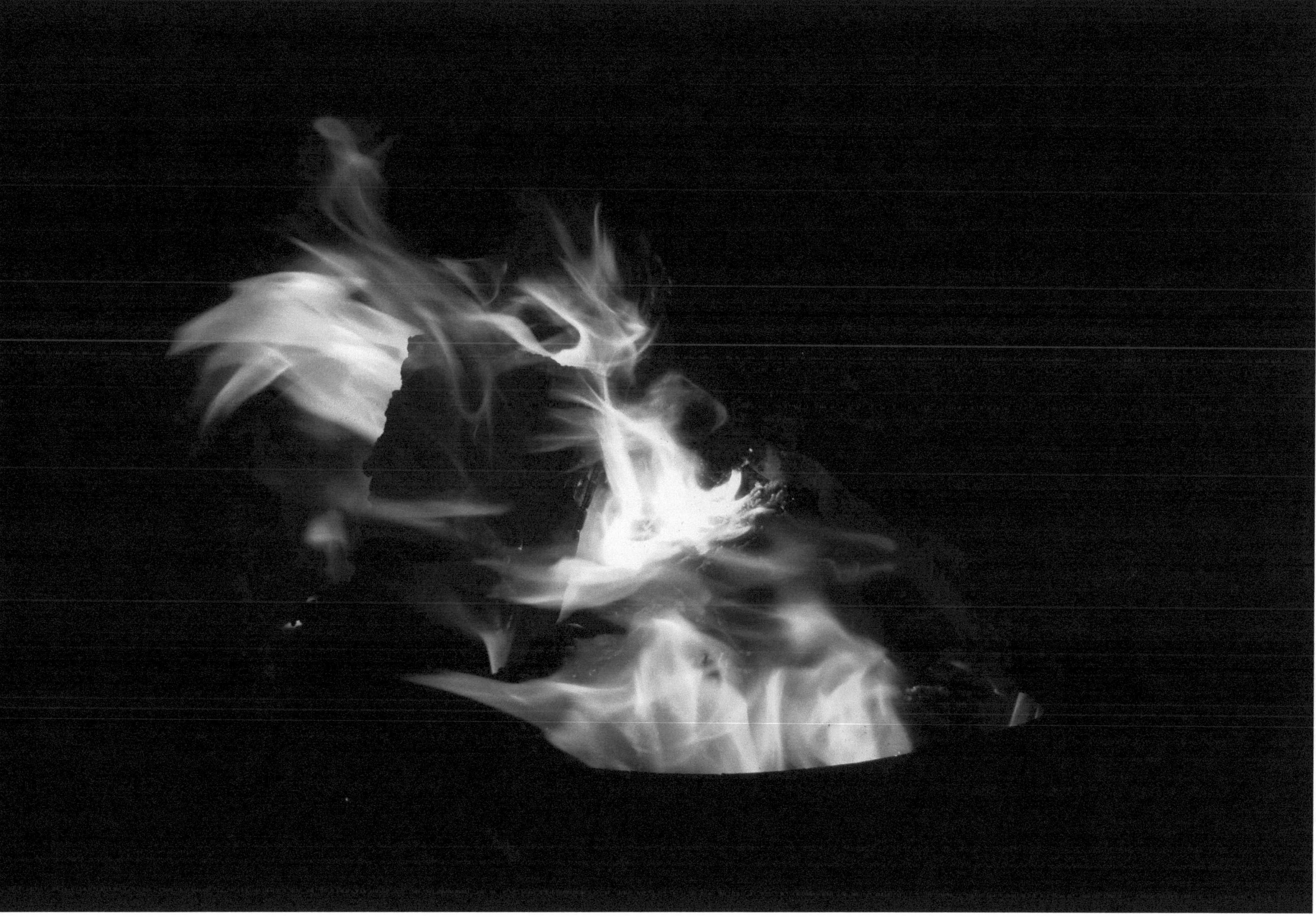

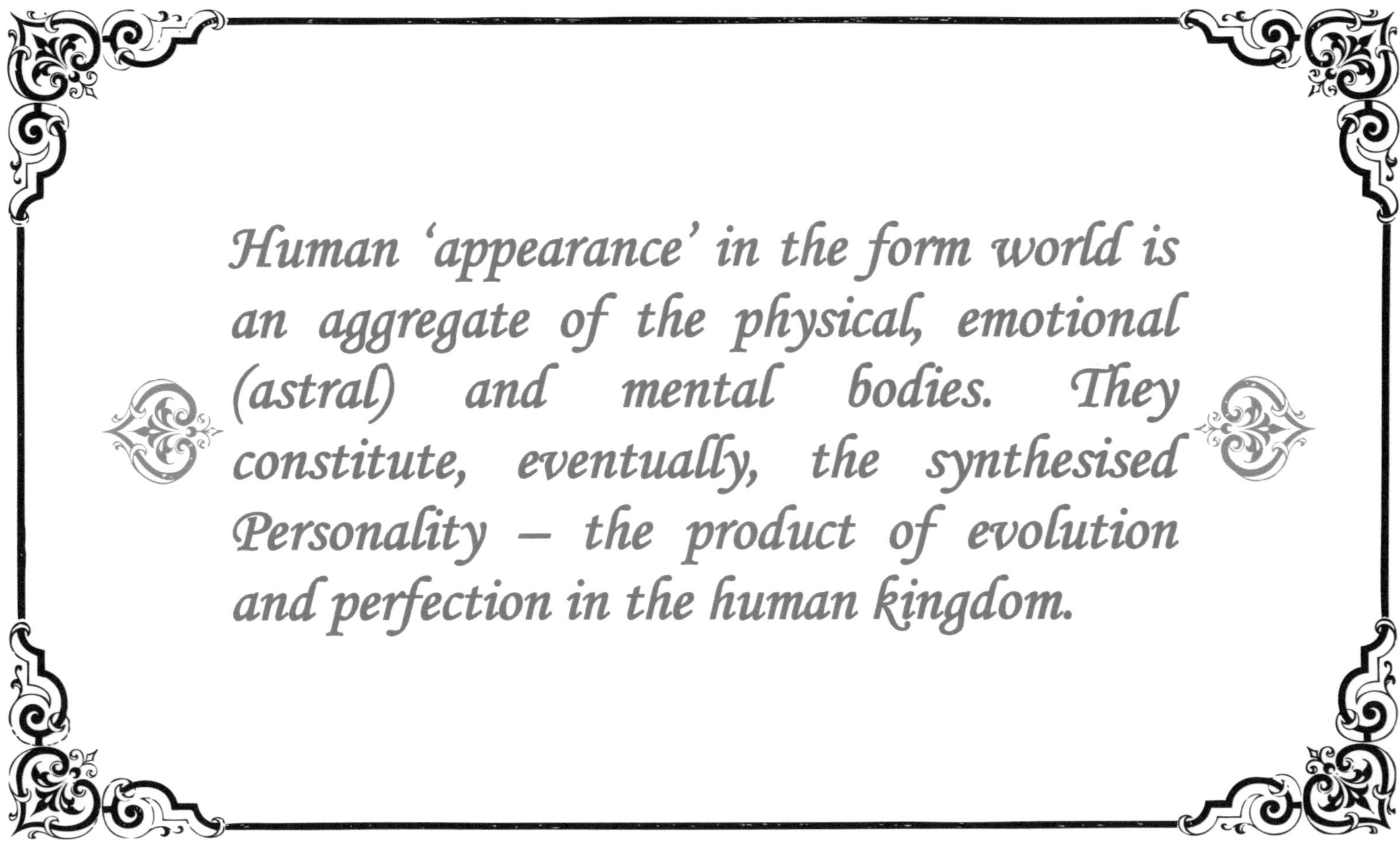

Human 'appearance' in the form world is an aggregate of the physical, emotional (astral) and mental bodies. They constitute, eventually, the synthesised Personality – the product of evolution and perfection in the human kingdom.

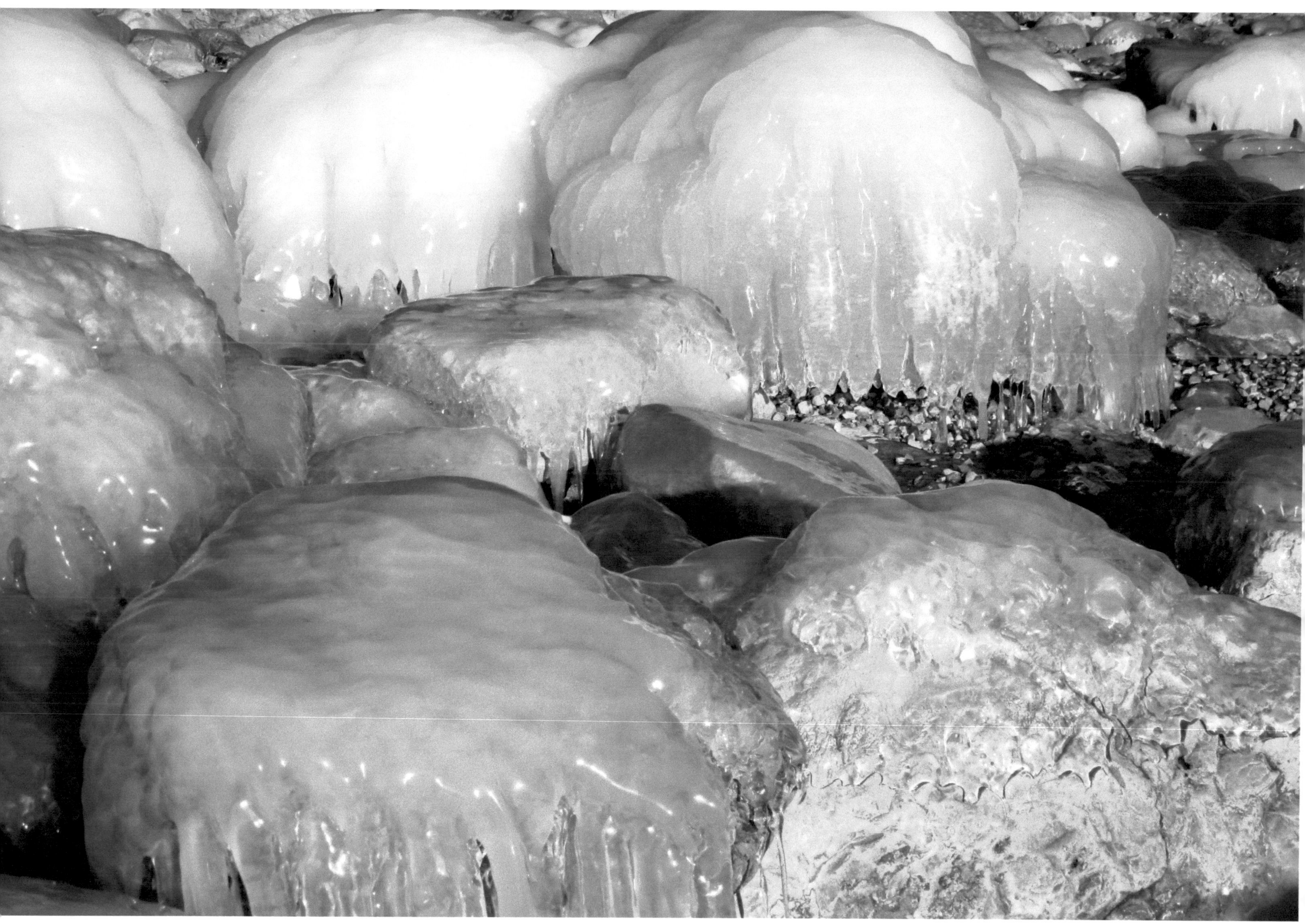

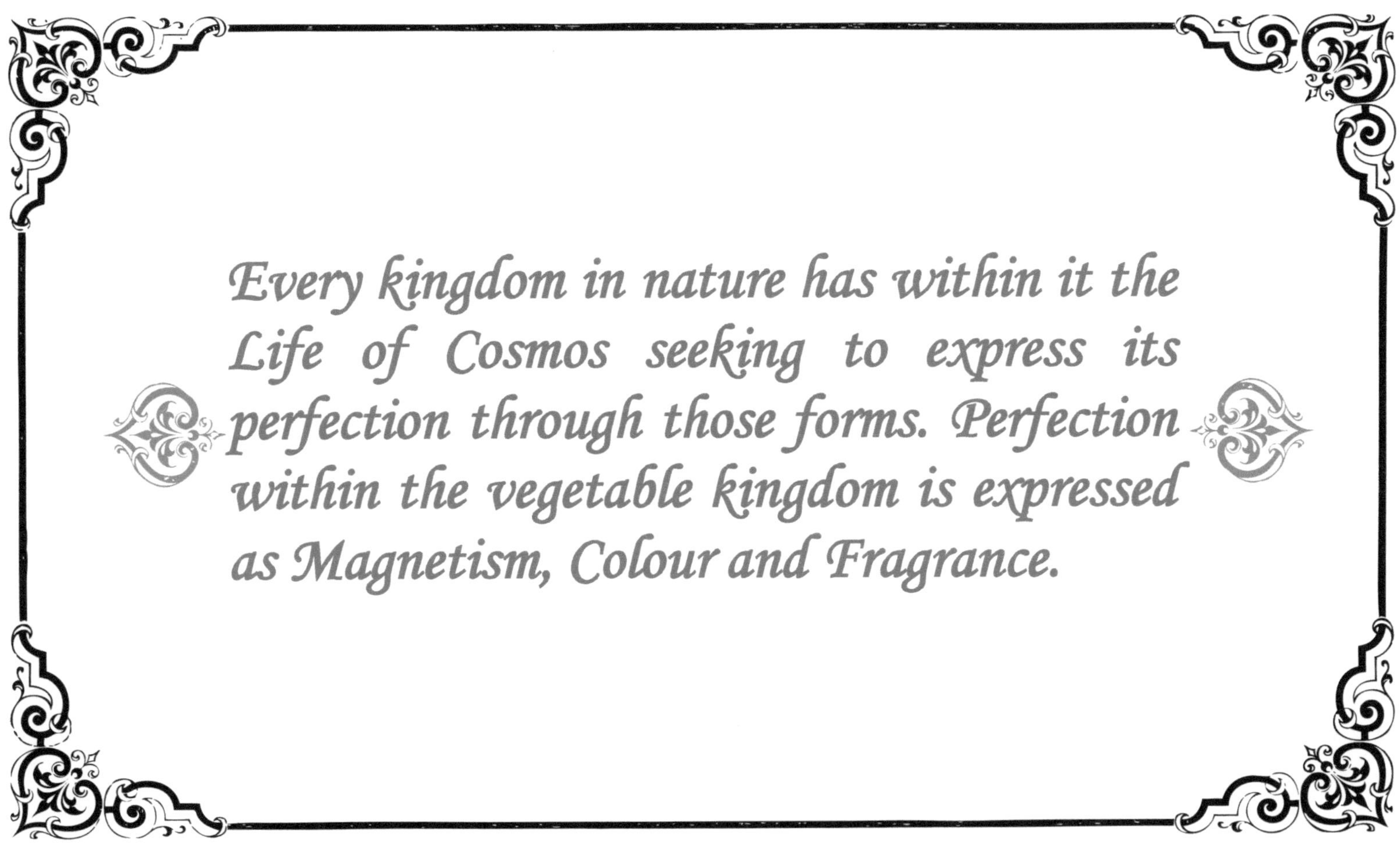

Every kingdom in nature has within it the Life of Cosmos seeking to express its perfection through those forms. Perfection within the vegetable kingdom is expressed as Magnetism, Colour and Fragrance.

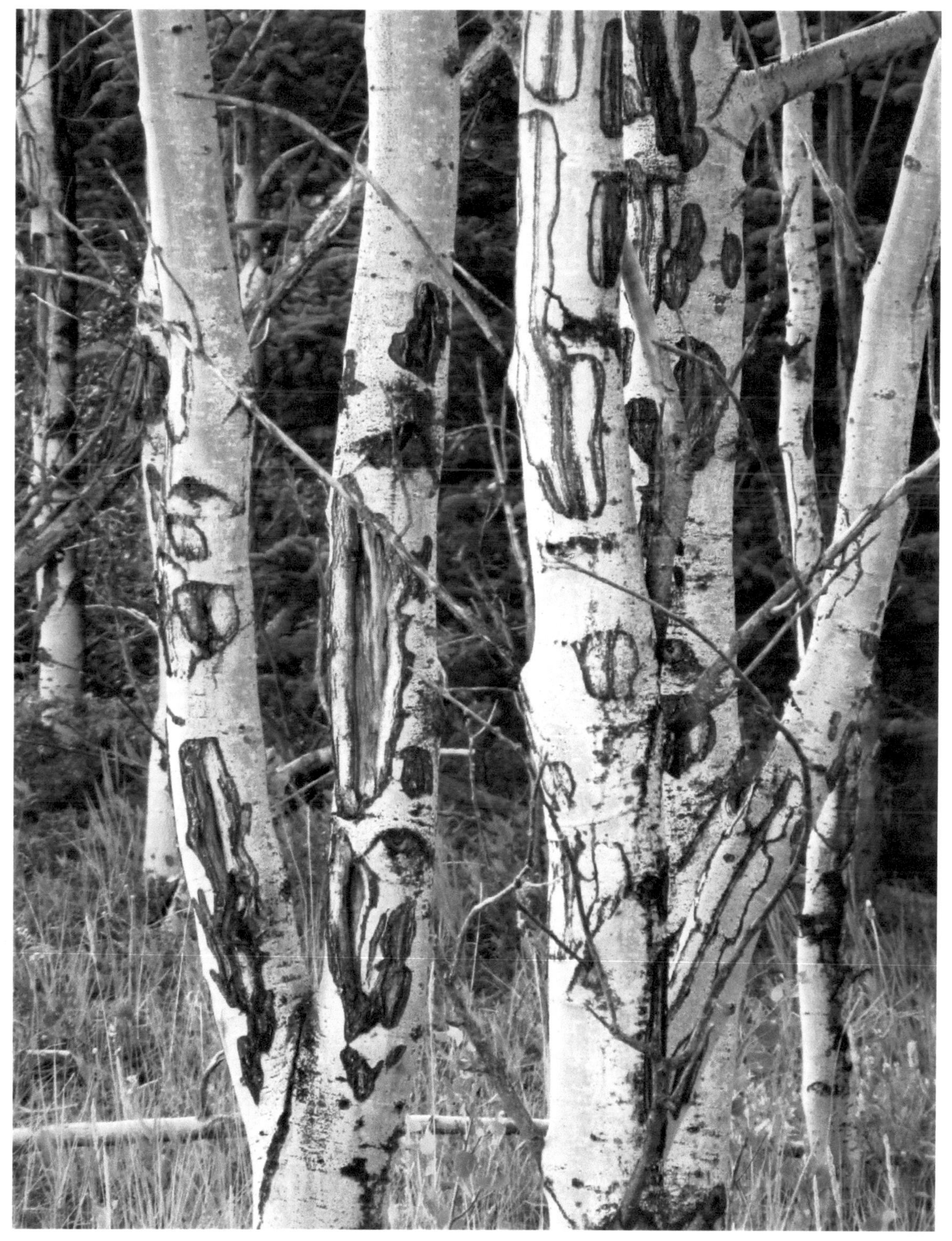

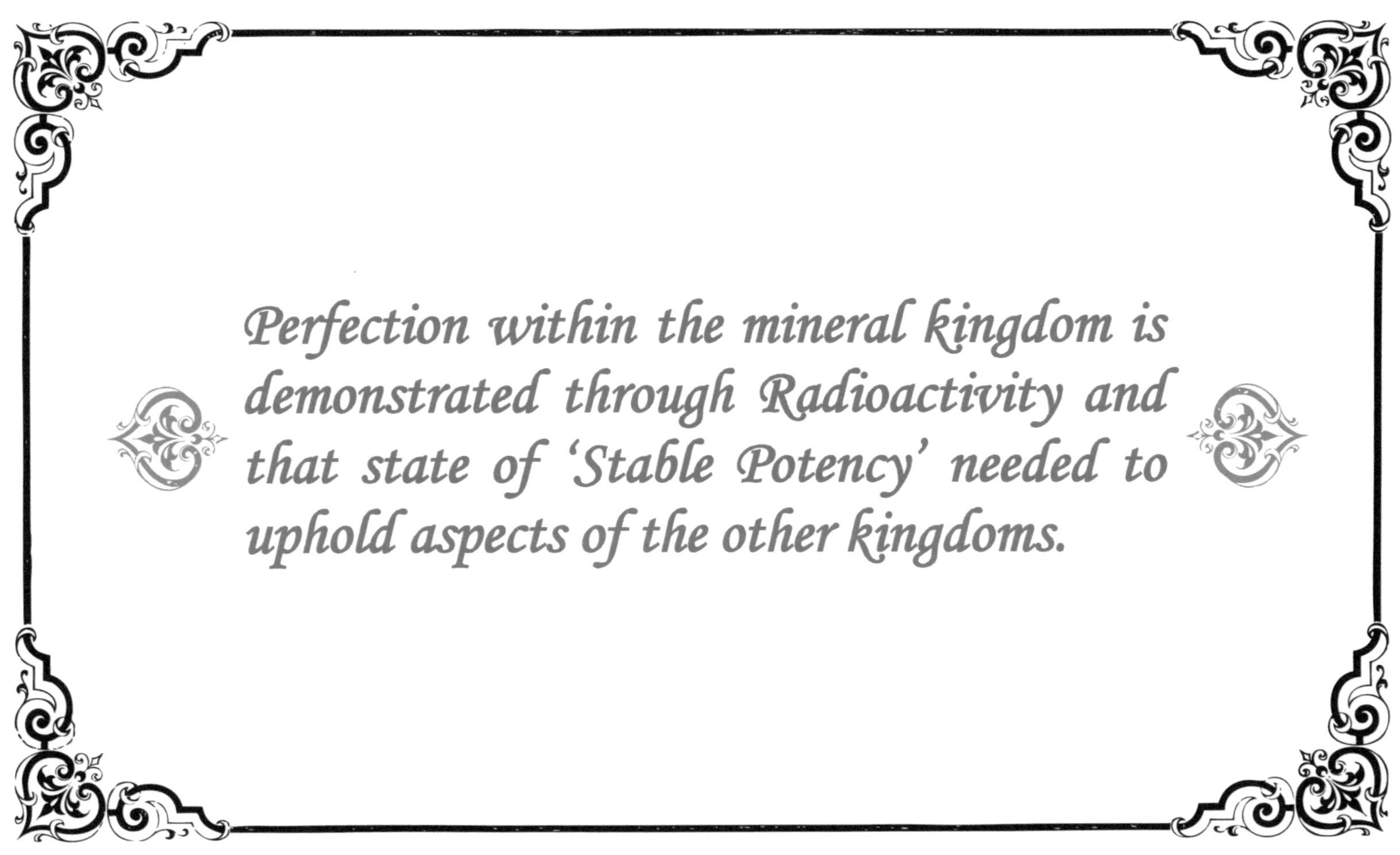

Perfection within the mineral kingdom is demonstrated through Radioactivity and that state of 'Stable Potency' needed to uphold aspects of the other kingdoms.

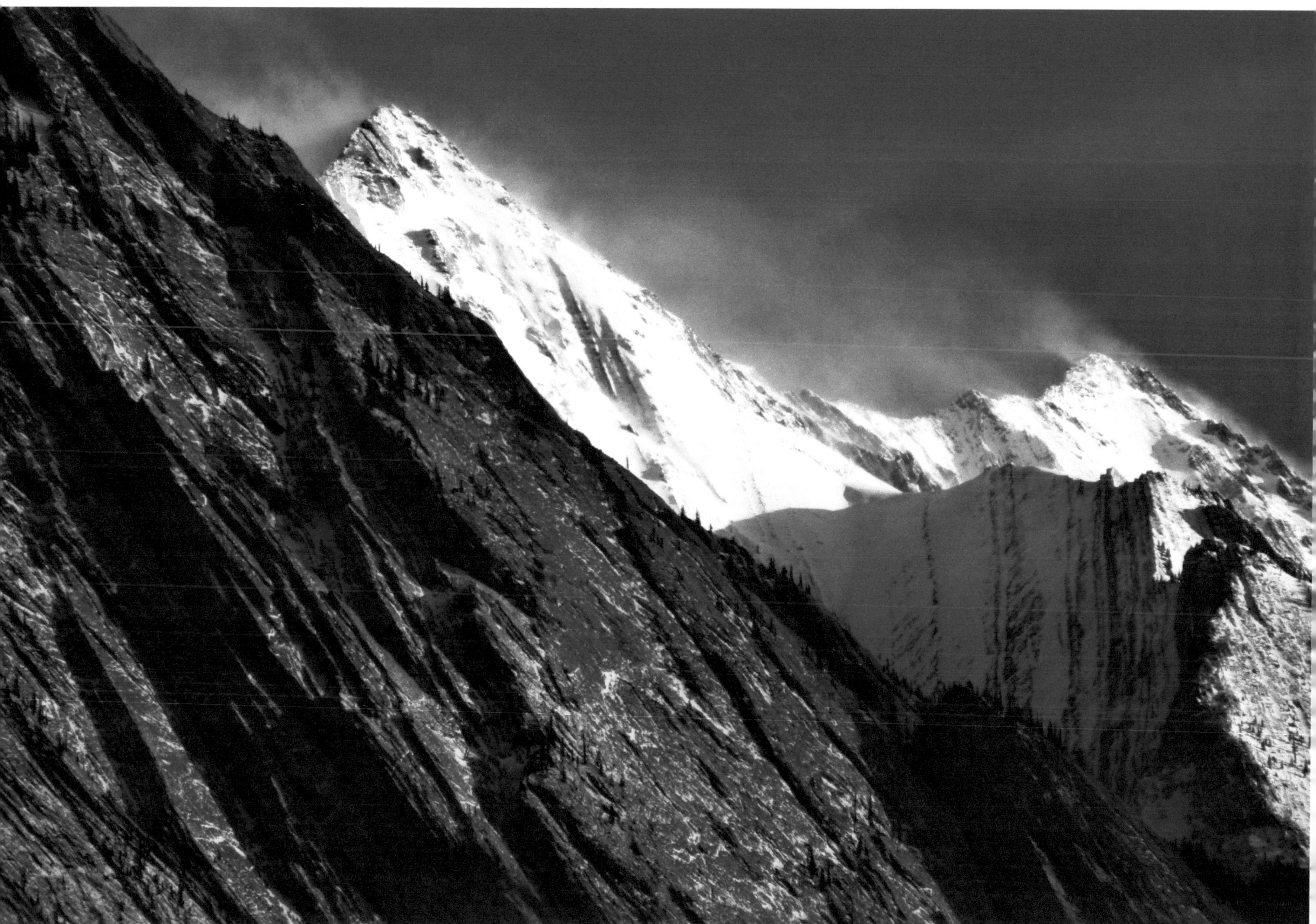

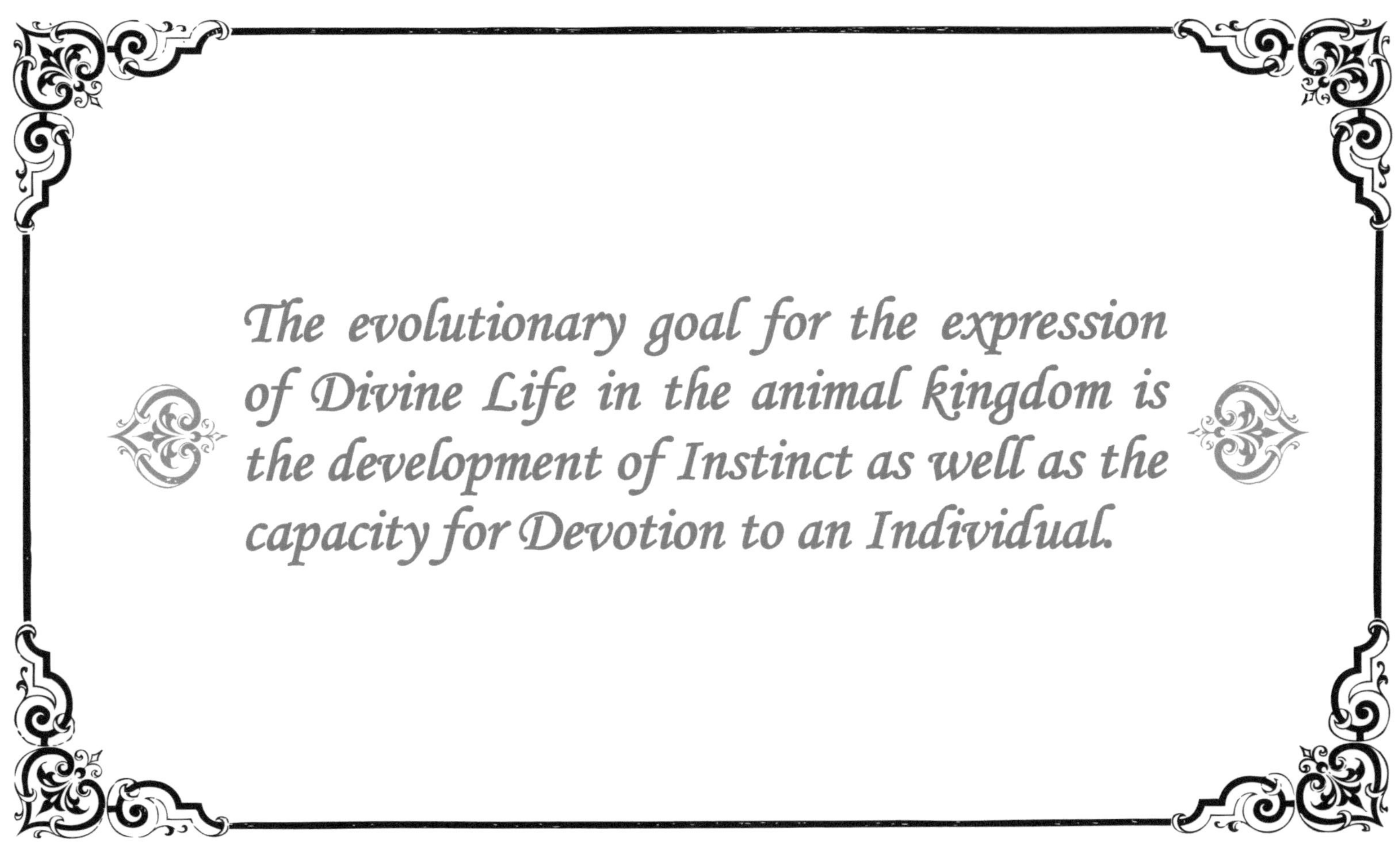

The evolutionary goal for the expression of Divine Life in the animal kingdom is the development of Instinct as well as the capacity for Devotion to an Individual.

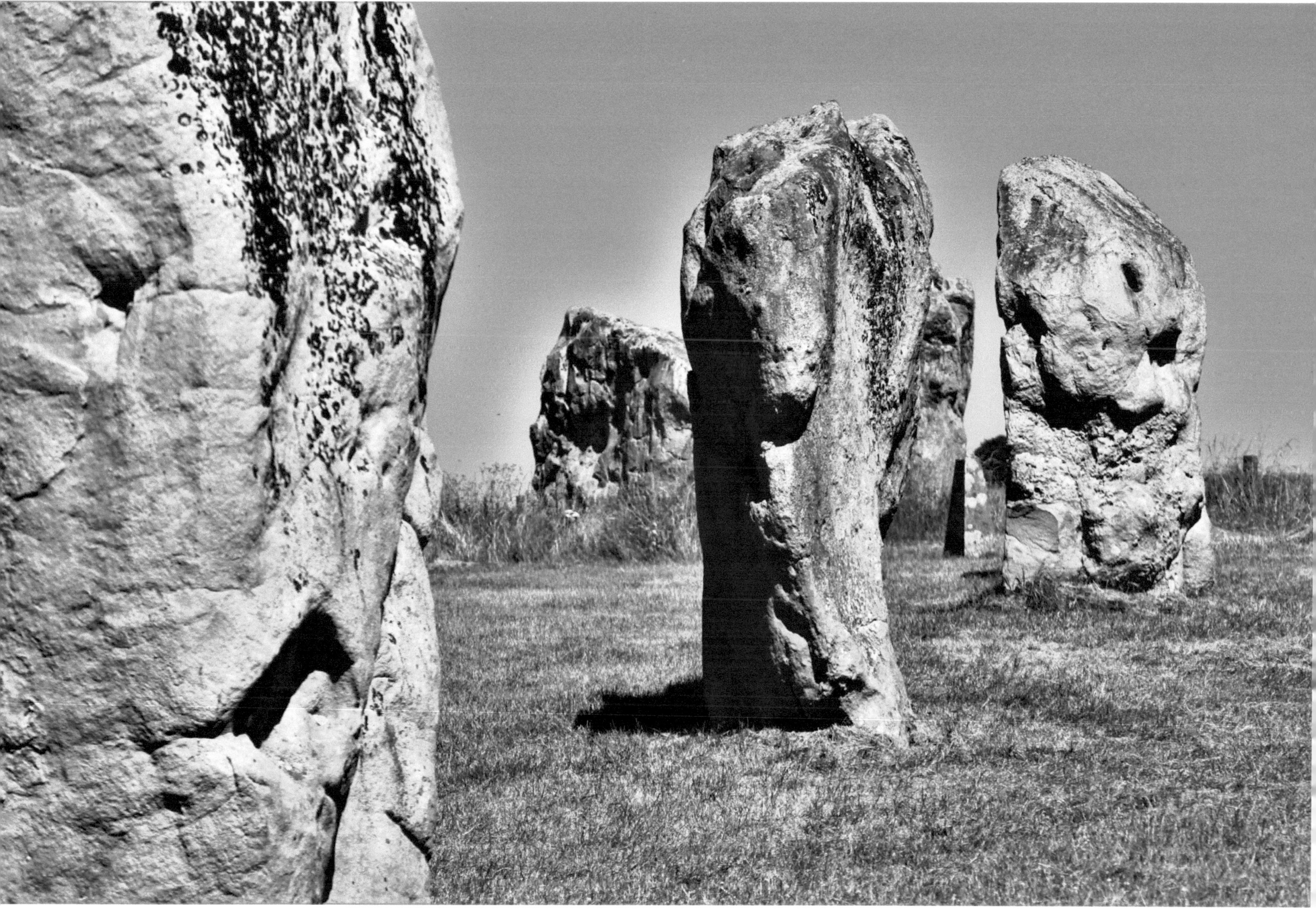

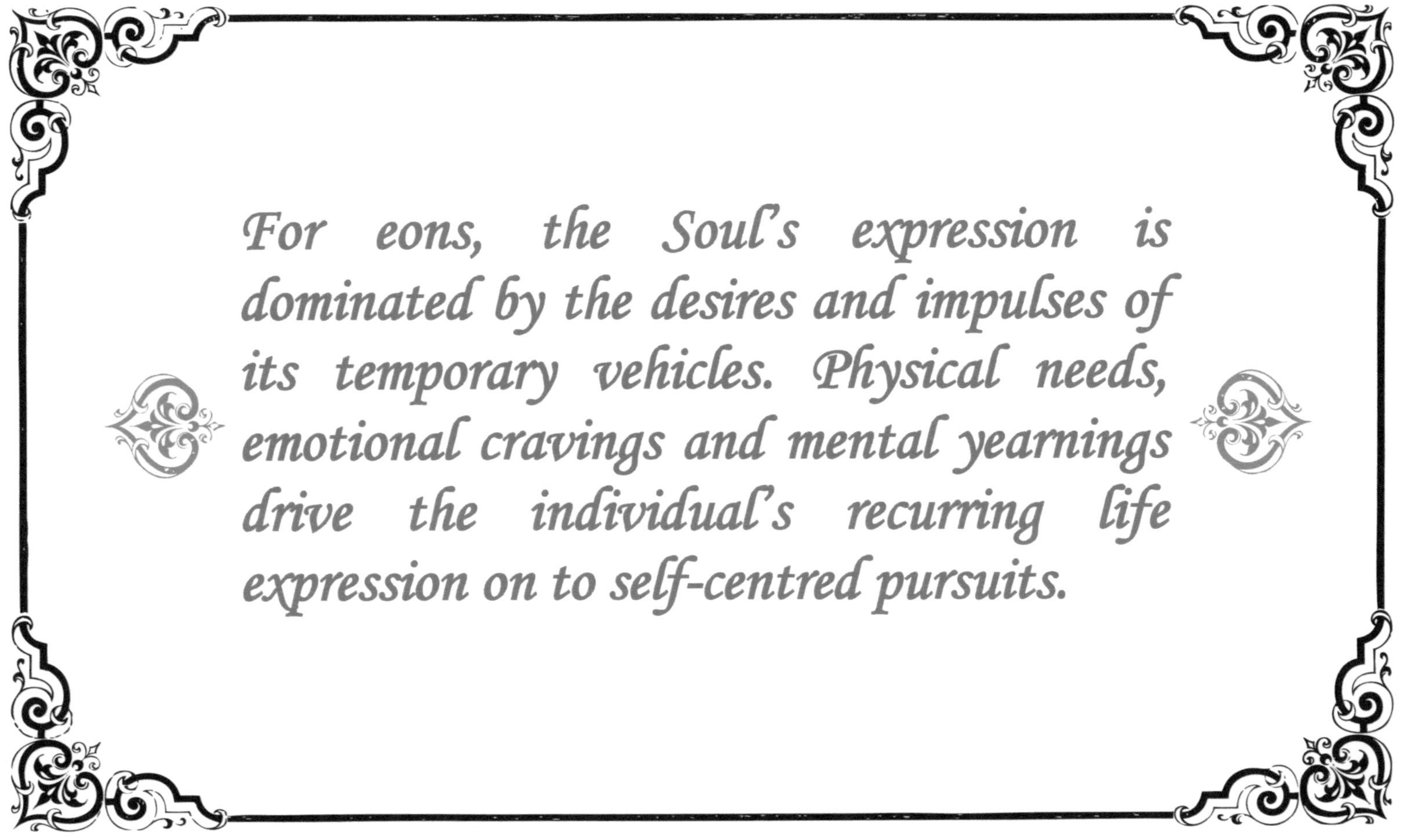

For eons, the Soul's expression is dominated by the desires and impulses of its temporary vehicles. Physical needs, emotional cravings and mental yearnings drive the individual's recurring life expression on to self-centred pursuits.

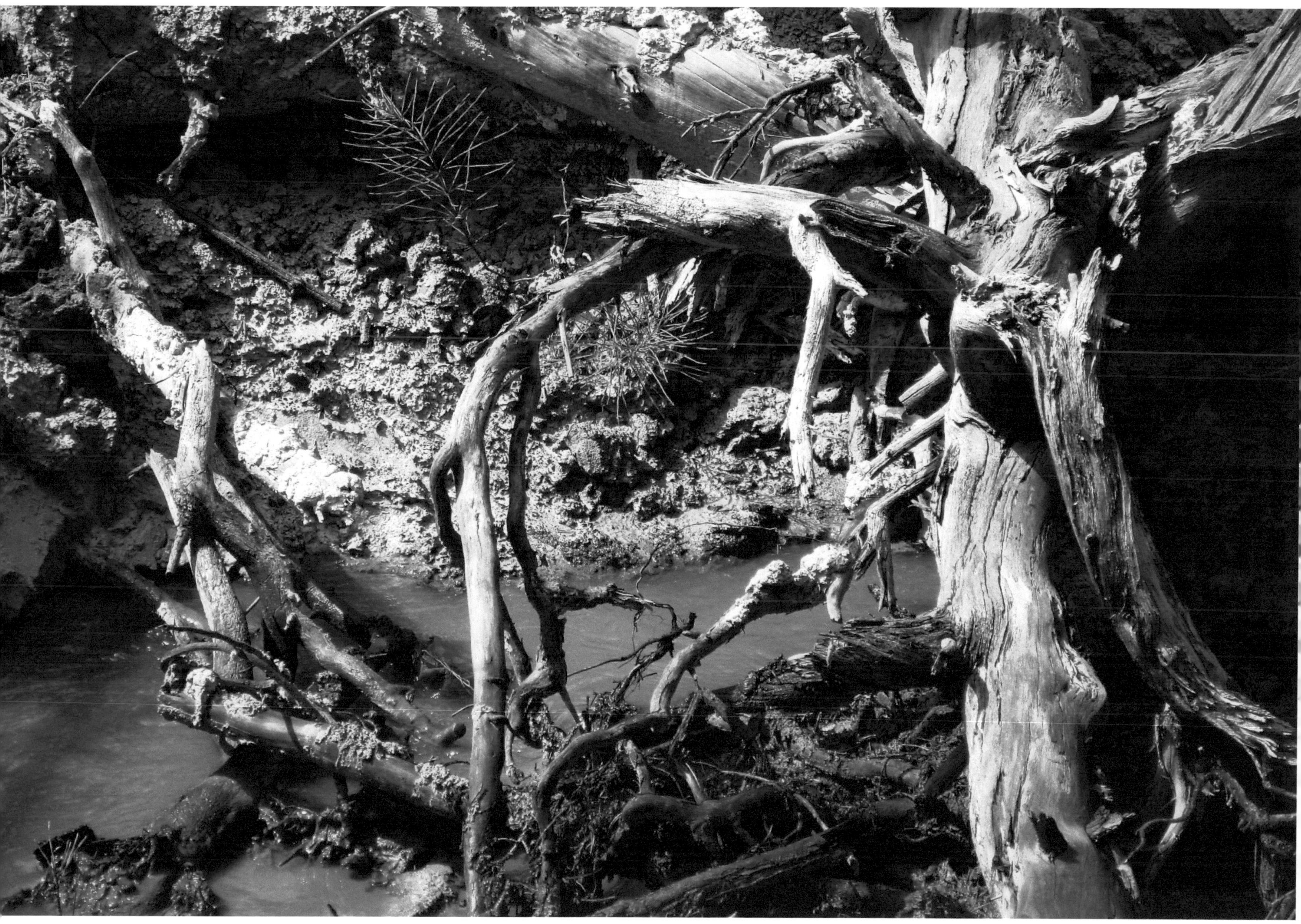

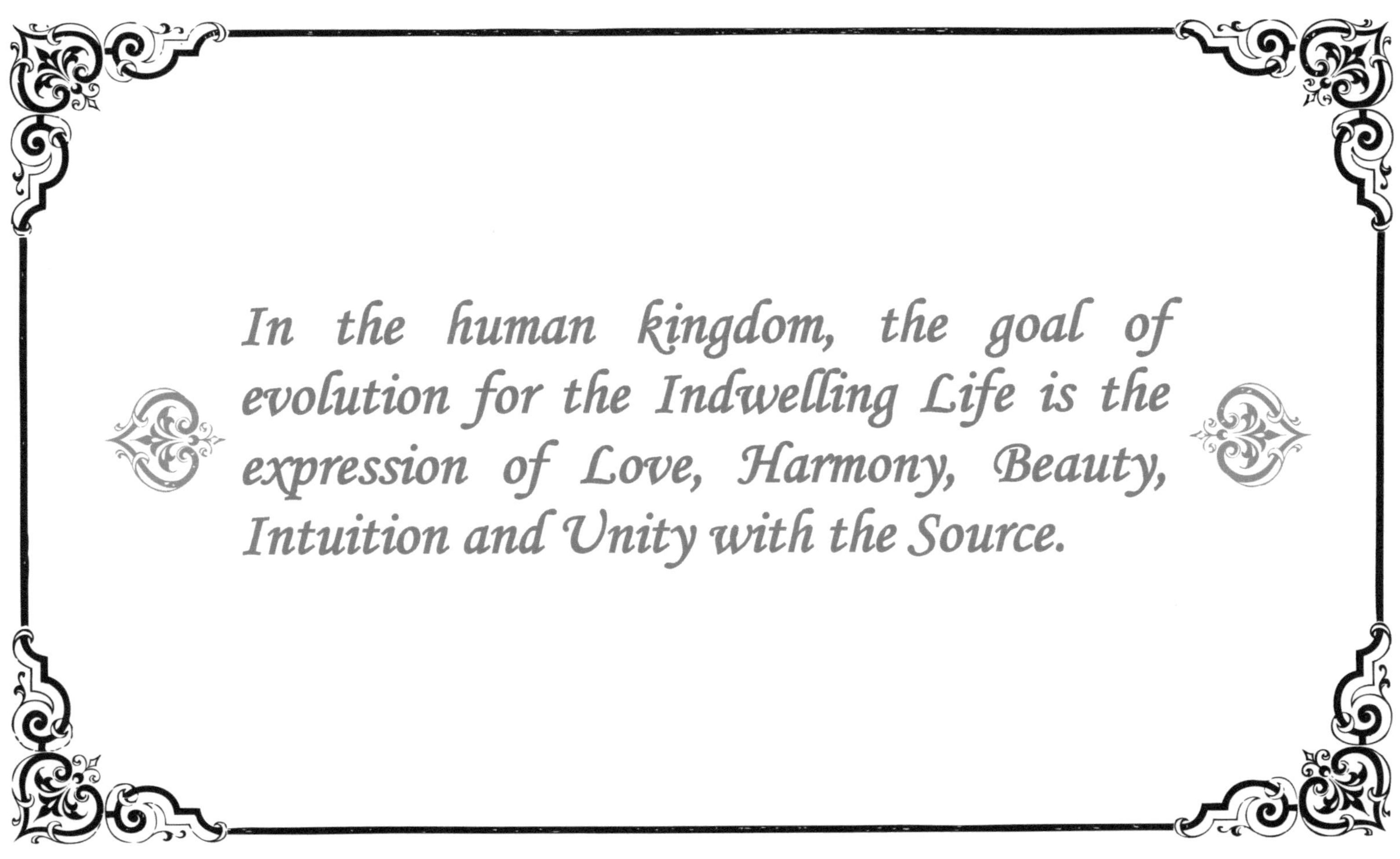

In the human kingdom, the goal of evolution for the Indwelling Life is the expression of Love, Harmony, Beauty, Intuition and Unity with the Source.

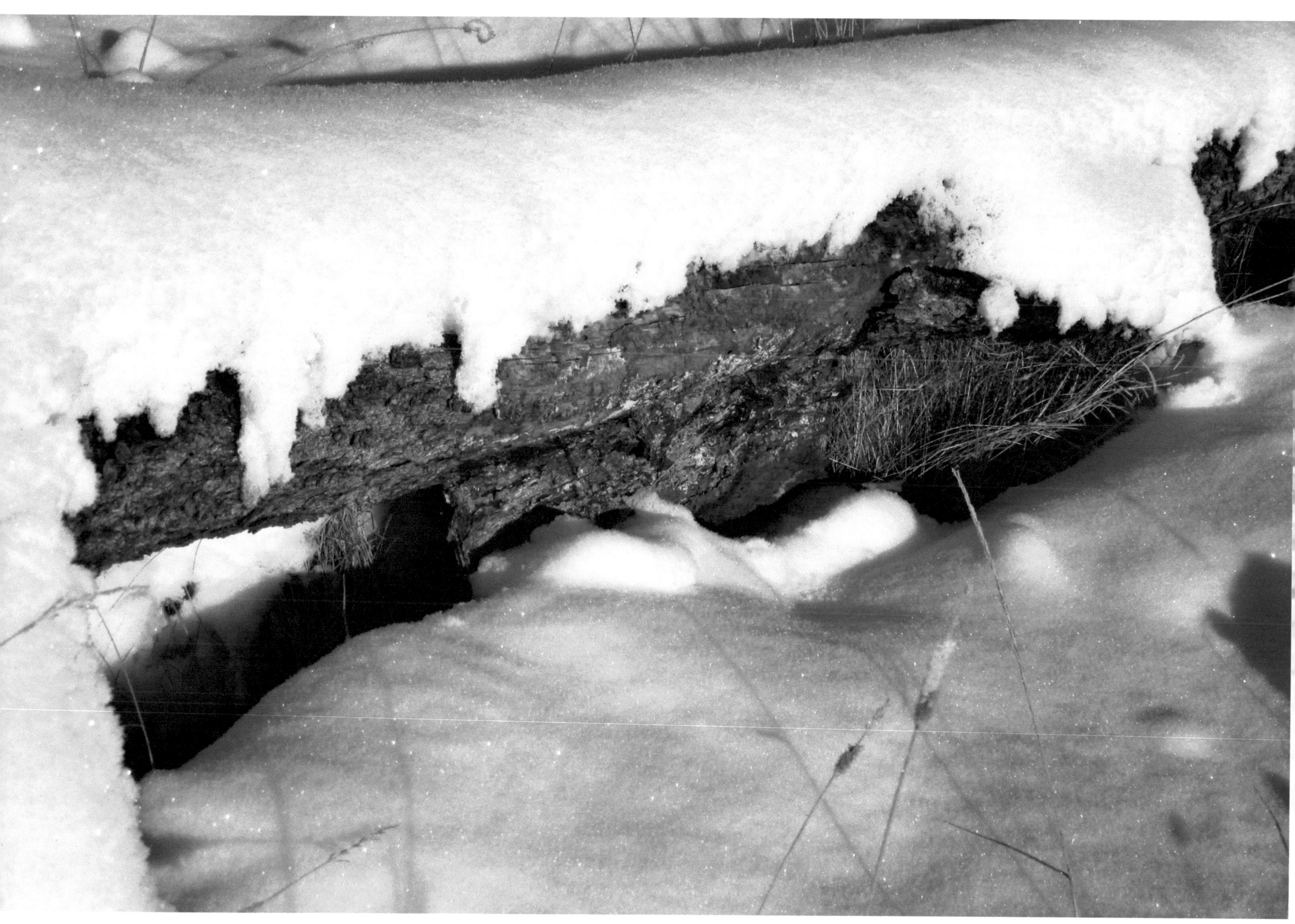

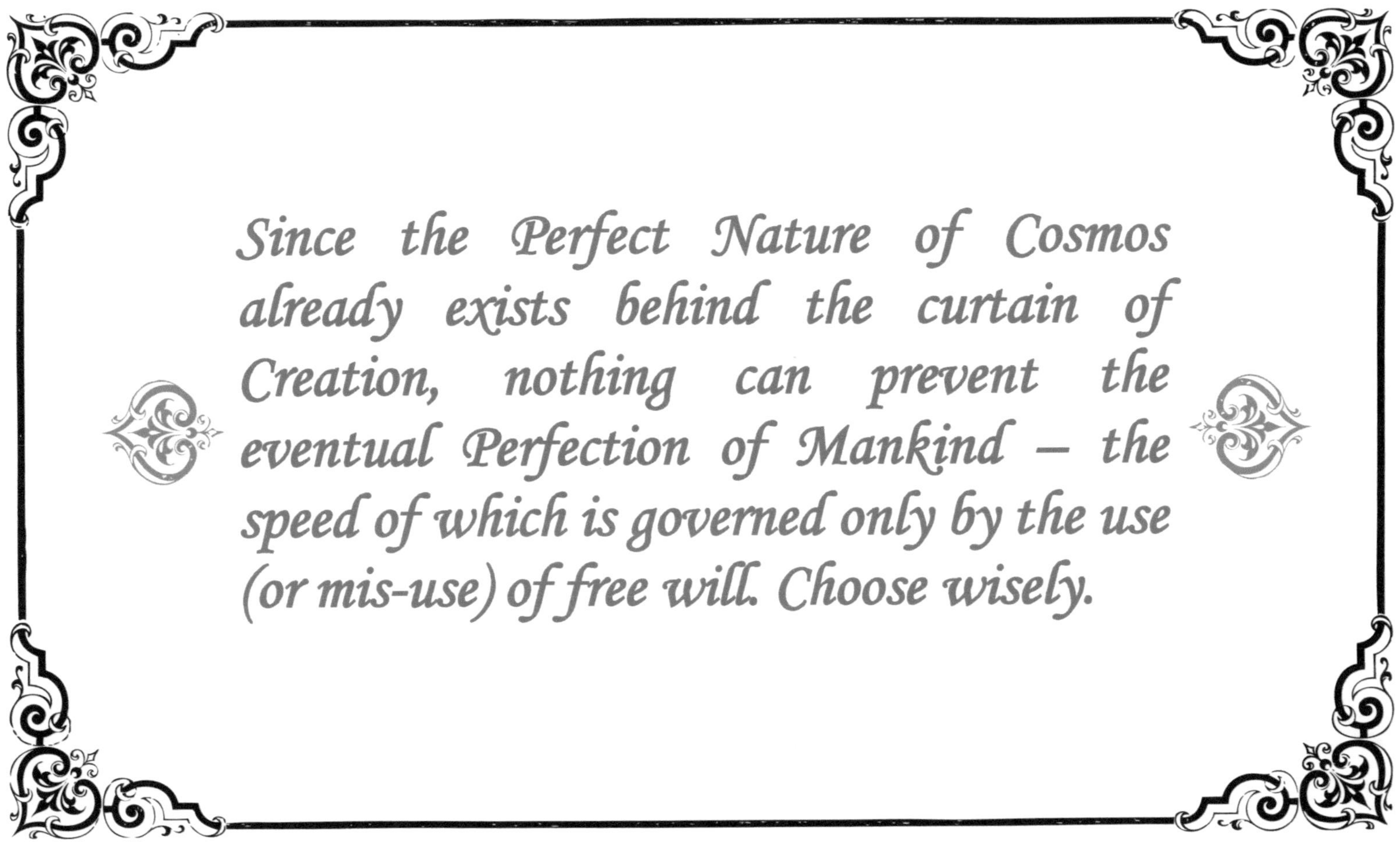

Since the Perfect Nature of Cosmos already exists behind the curtain of Creation, nothing can prevent the eventual Perfection of Mankind – the speed of which is governed only by the use (or mis-use) of free will. Choose wisely.

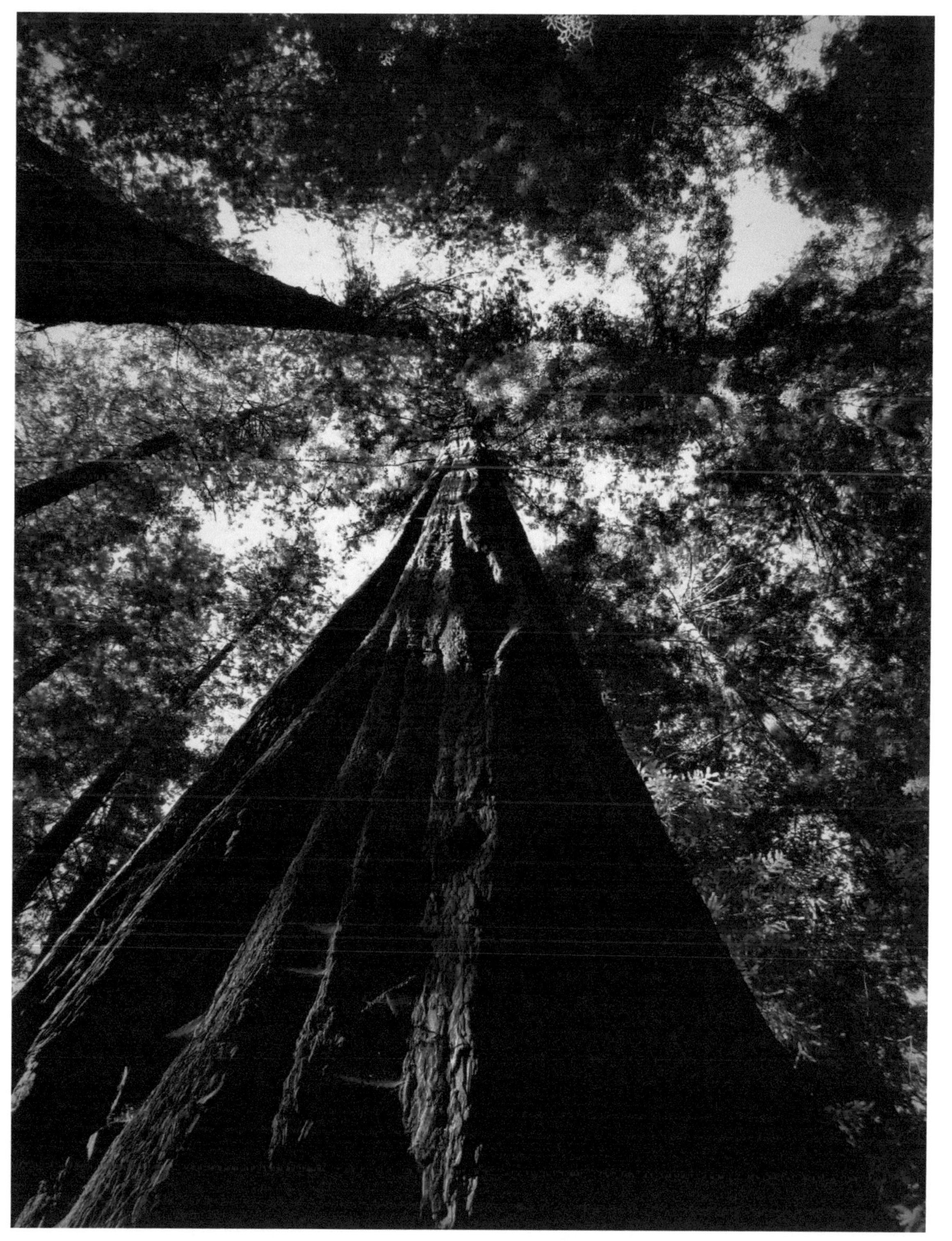

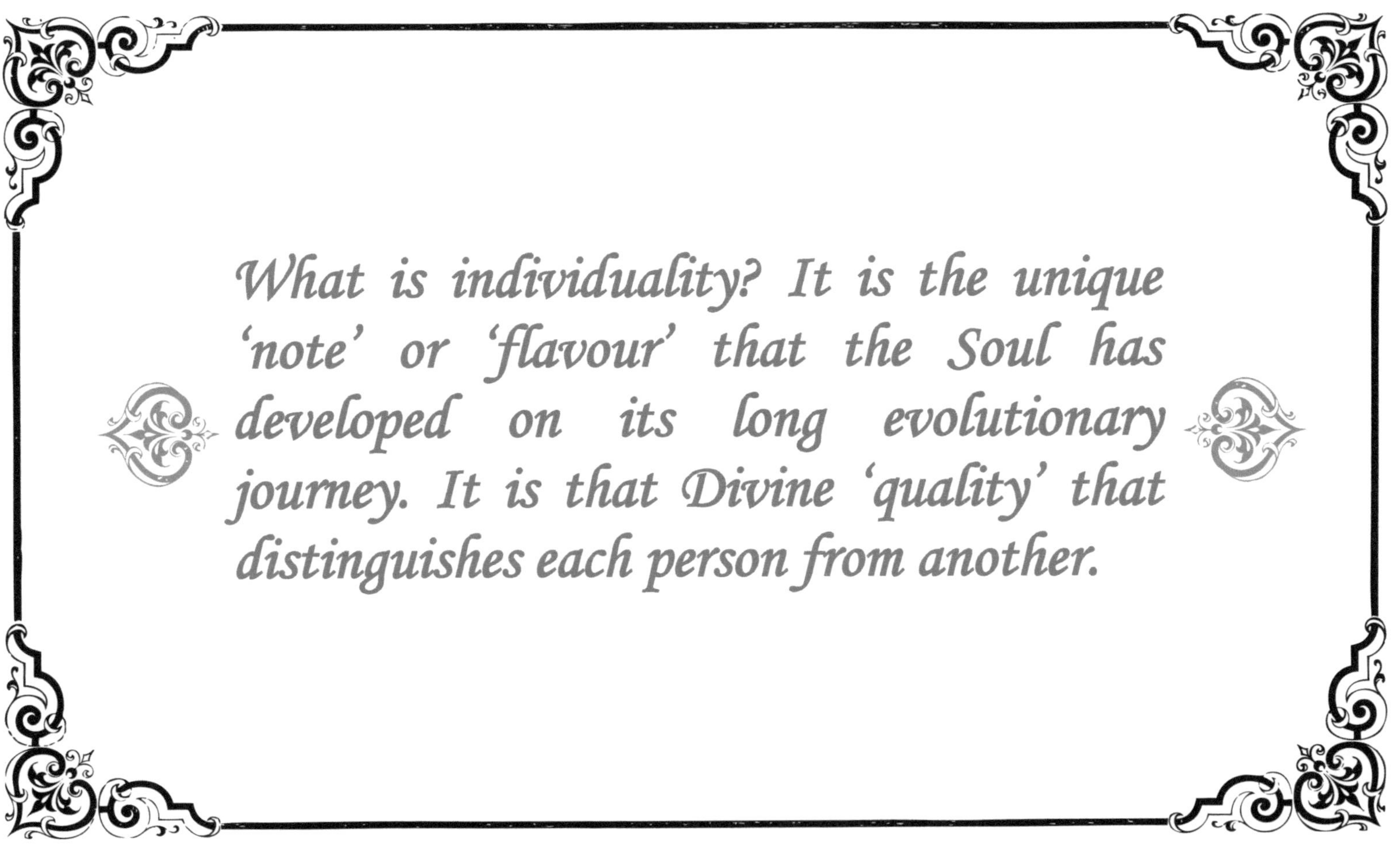

What is individuality? It is the unique 'note' or 'flavour' that the Soul has developed on its long evolutionary journey. It is that Divine 'quality' that distinguishes each person from another.

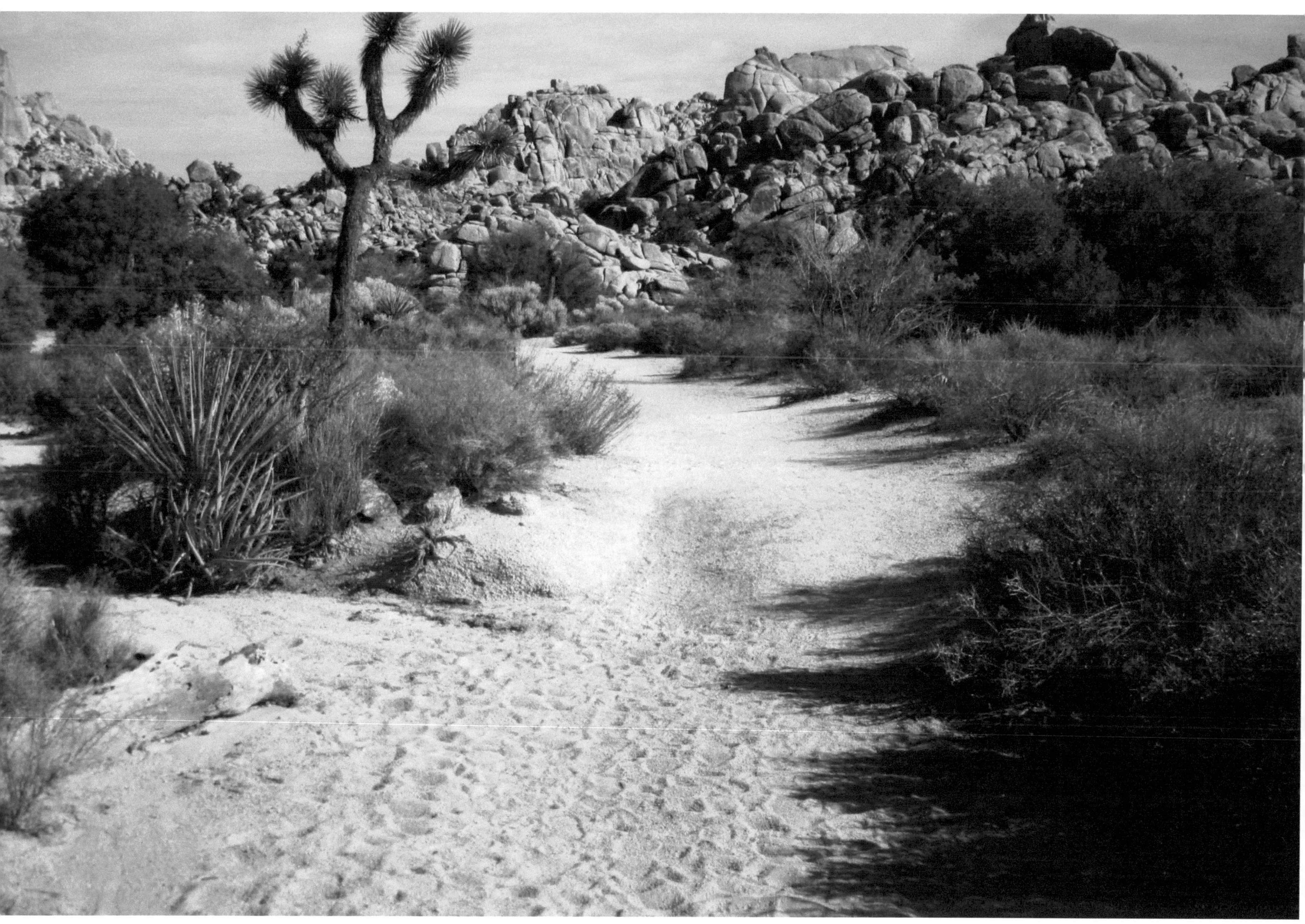

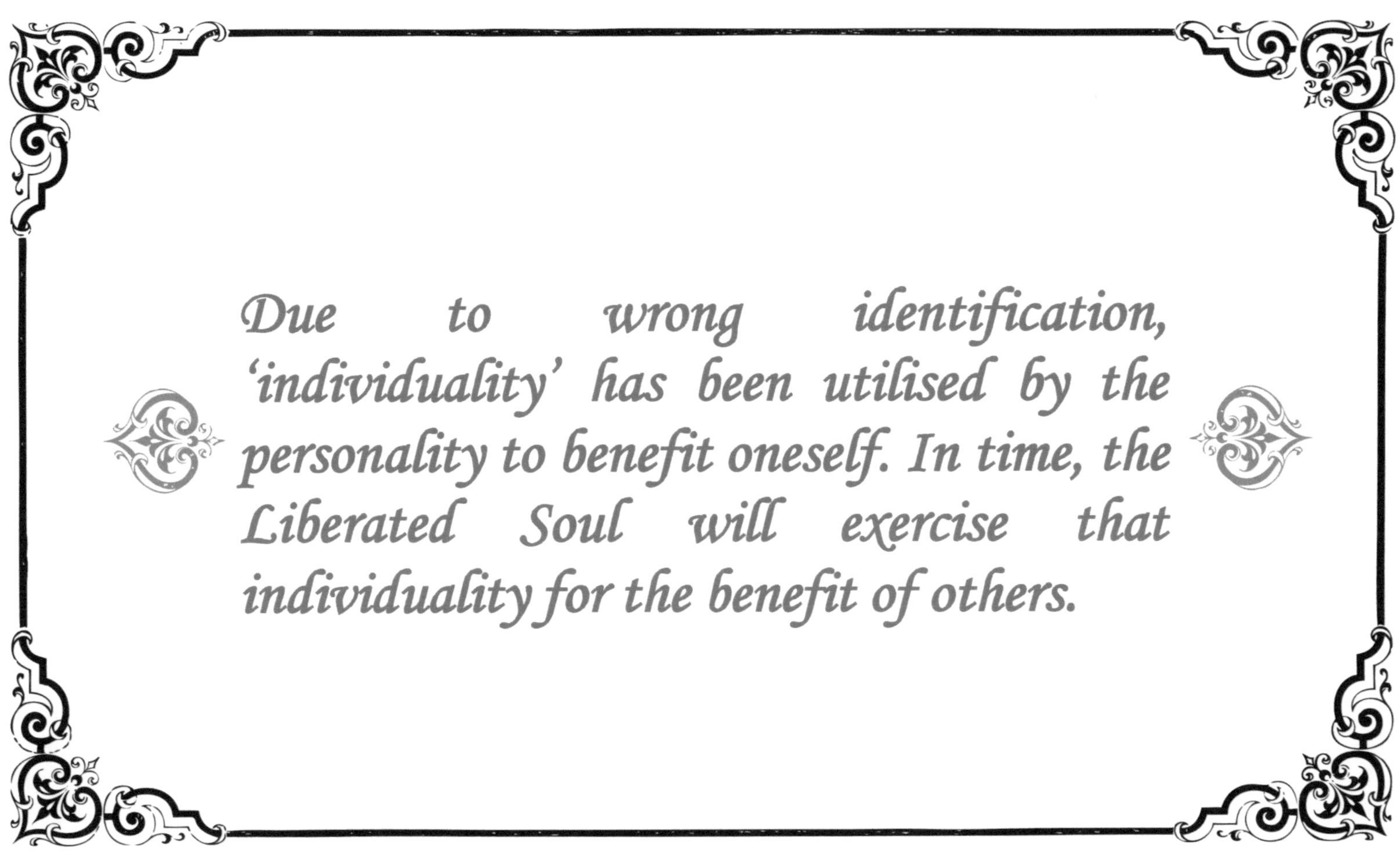

Due to wrong identification, 'individuality' has been utilised by the personality to benefit oneself. In time, the Liberated Soul will exercise that individuality for the benefit of others.

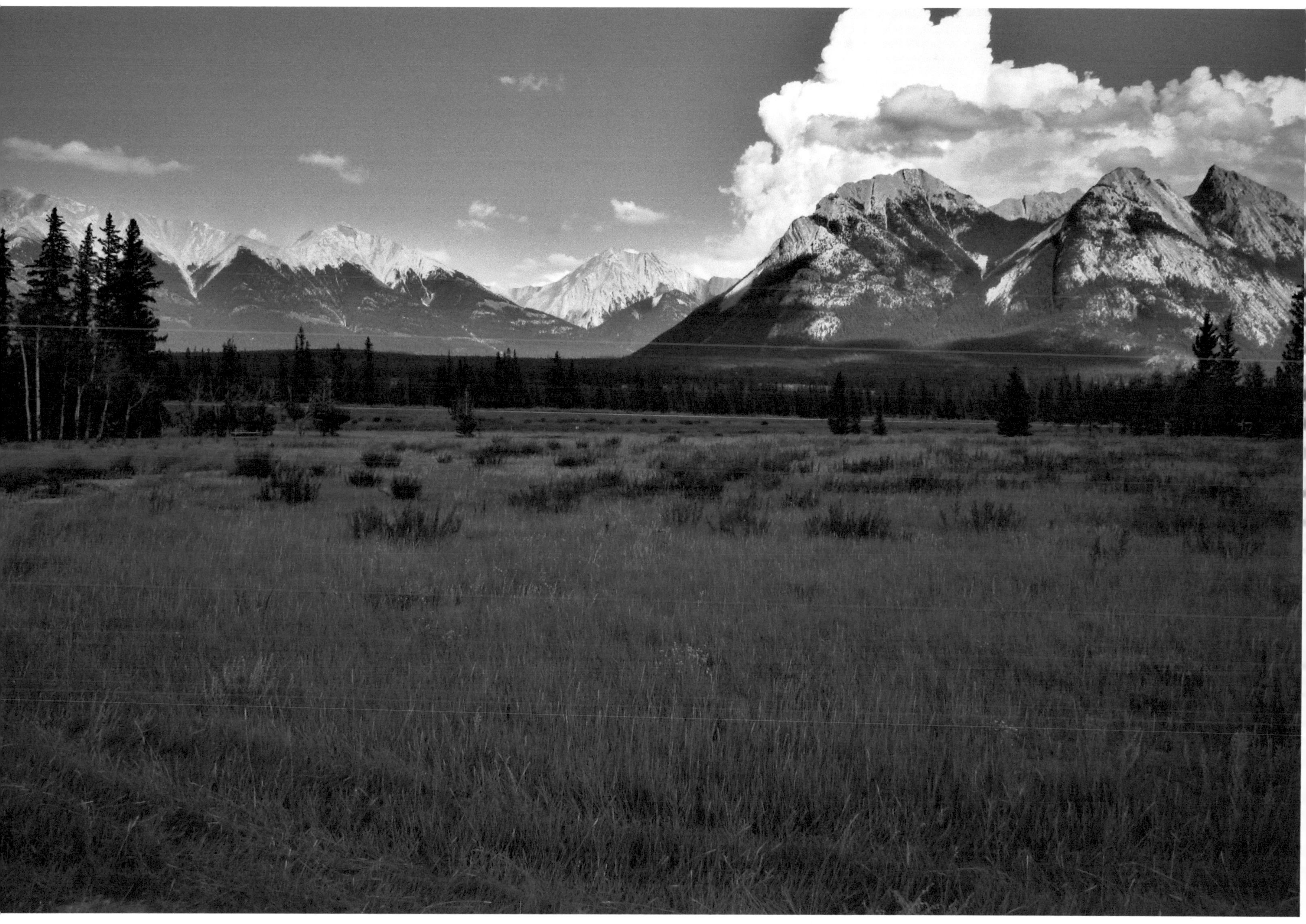

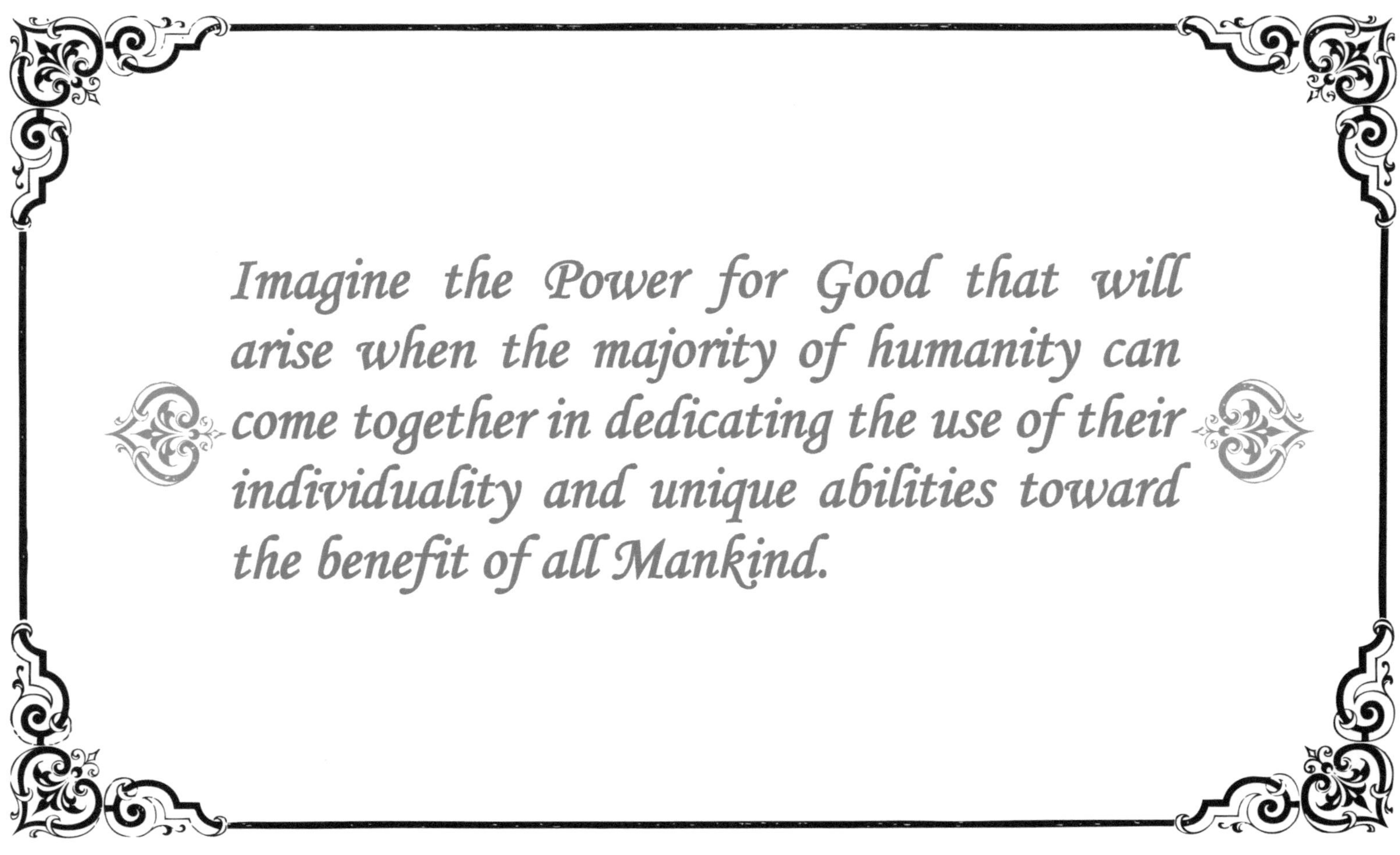

Imagine the Power for Good that will arise when the majority of humanity can come together in dedicating the use of their individuality and unique abilities toward the benefit of all Mankind.

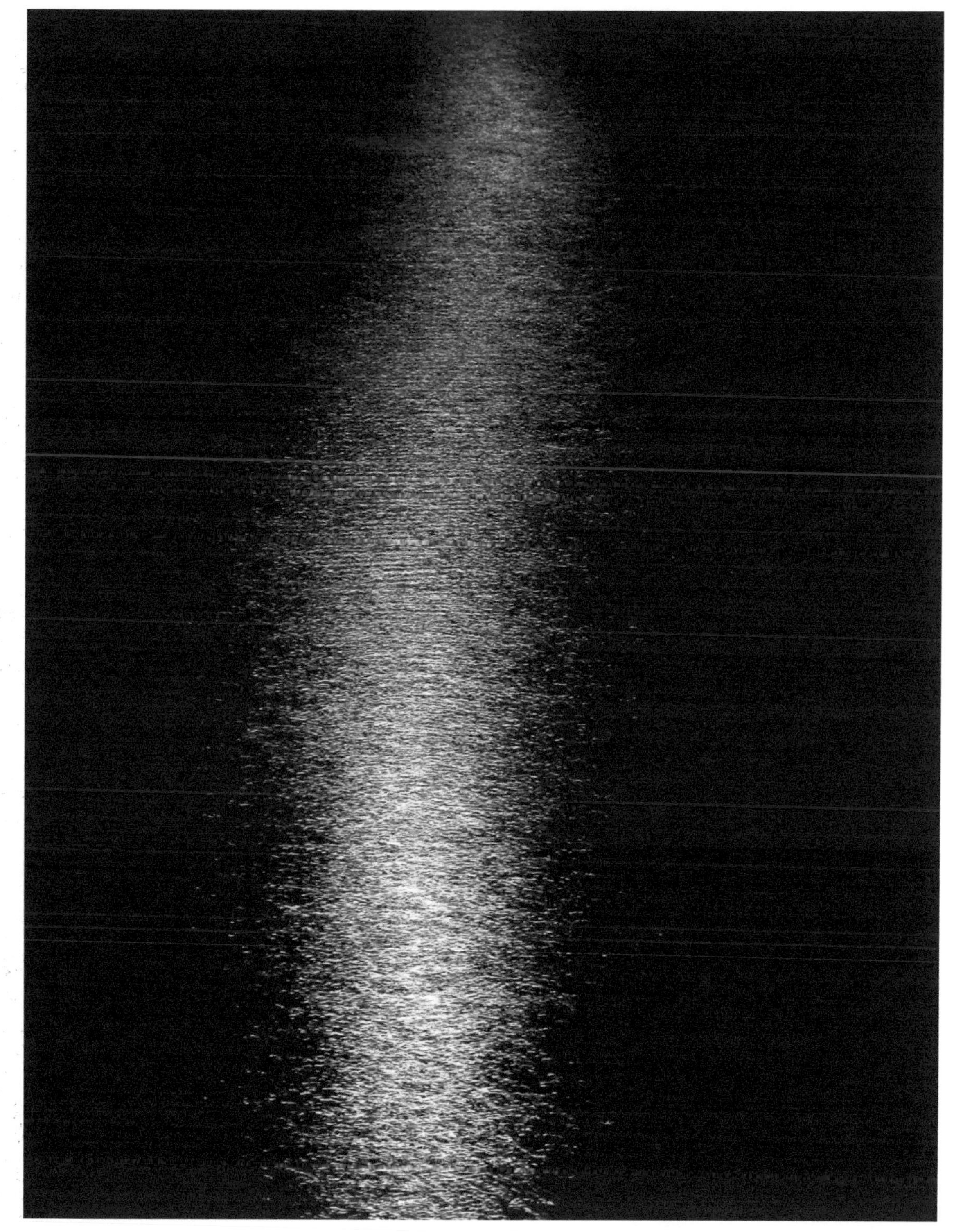

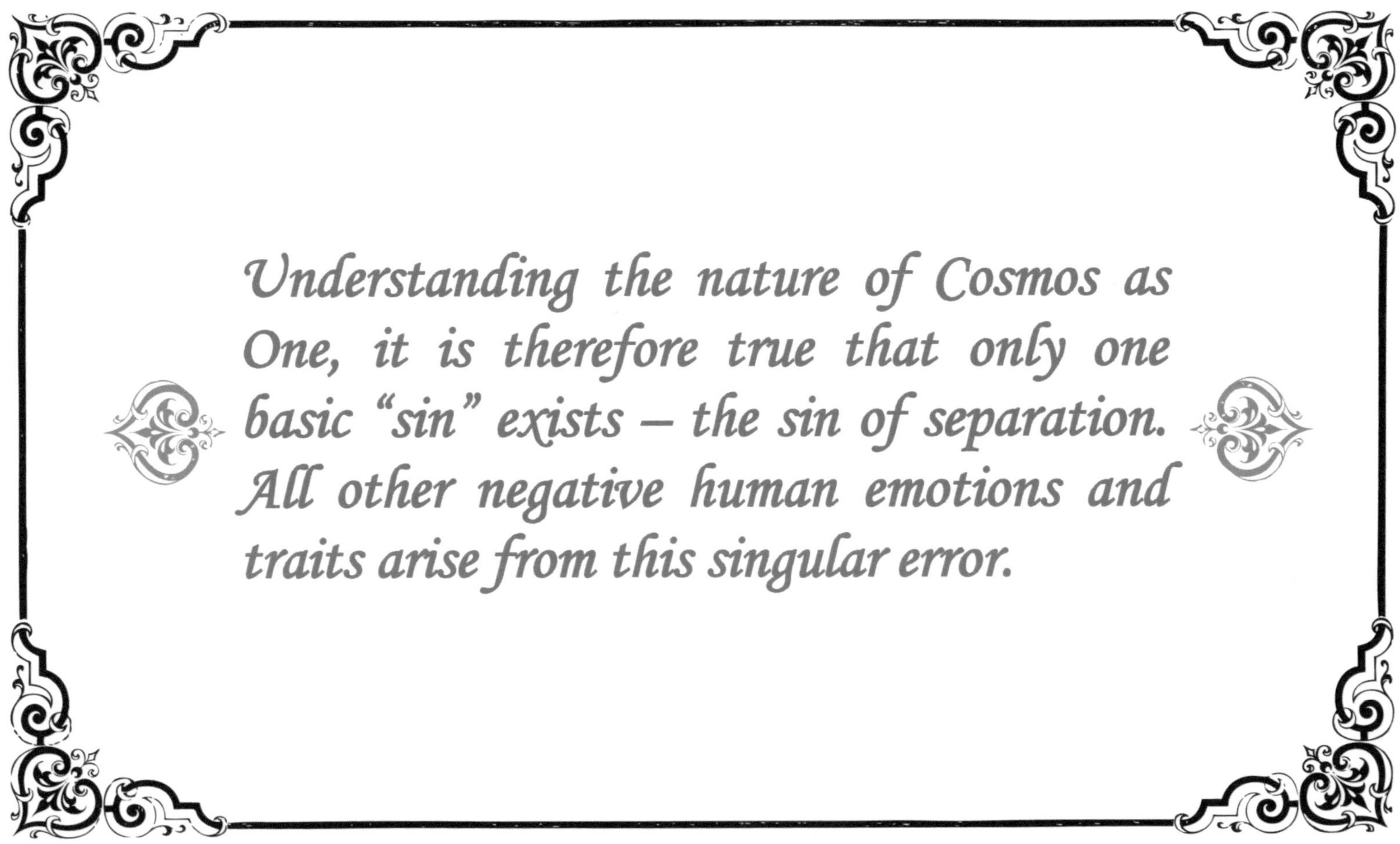

Understanding the nature of Cosmos as One, it is therefore true that only one basic "sin" exists – the sin of separation. All other negative human emotions and traits arise from this singular error.

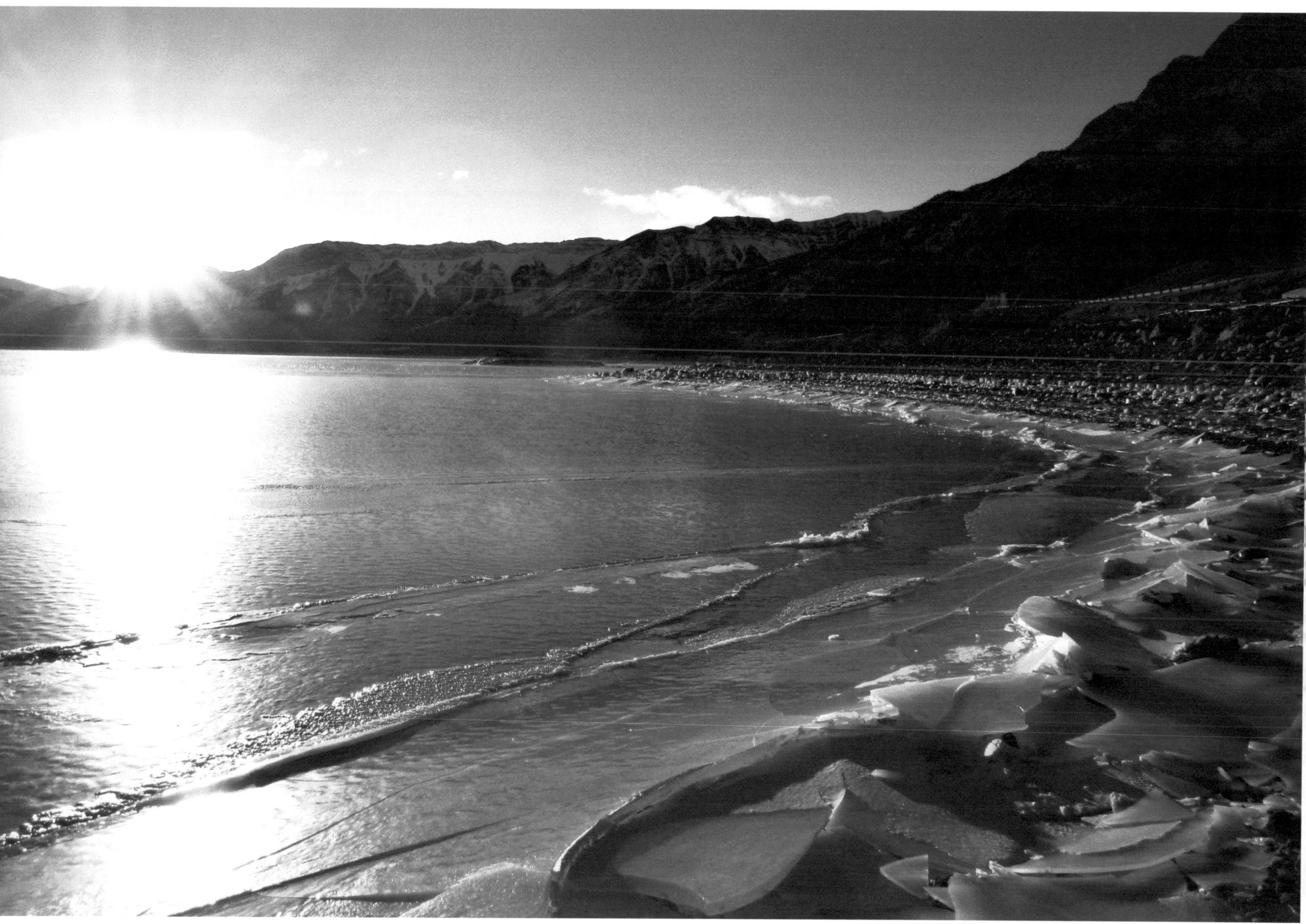

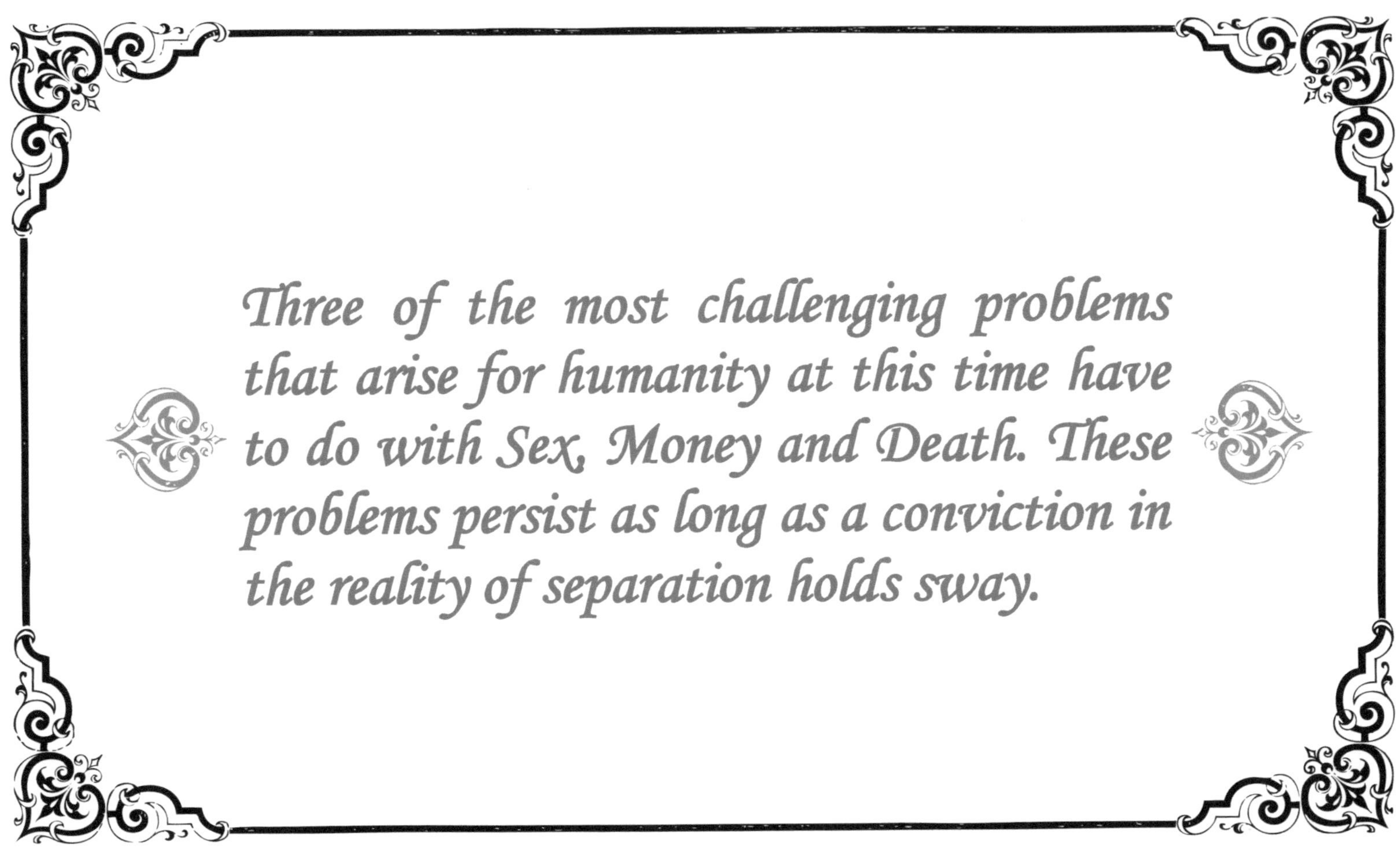

Three of the most challenging problems that arise for humanity at this time have to do with Sex, Money and Death. These problems persist as long as a conviction in the reality of separation holds sway.

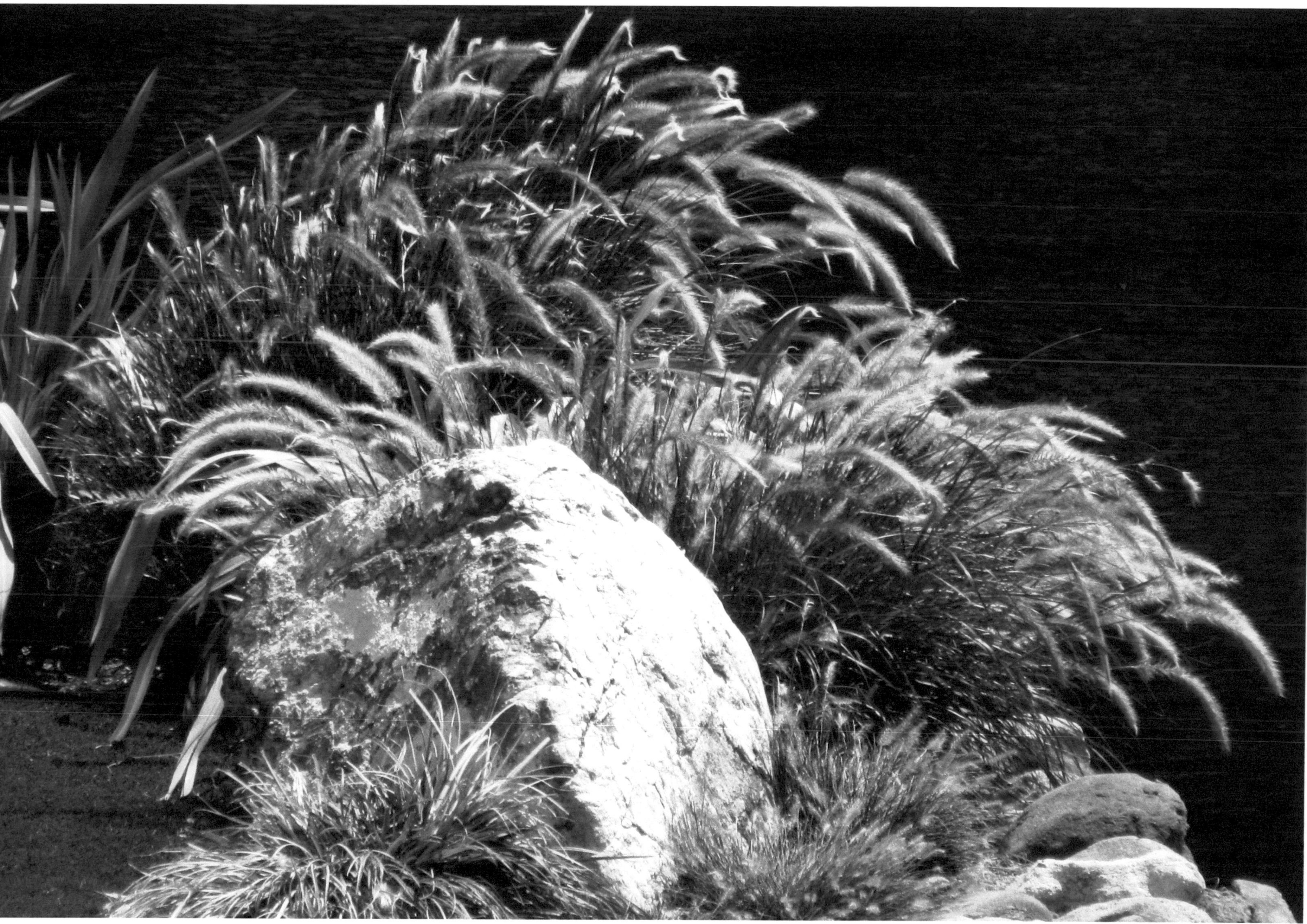

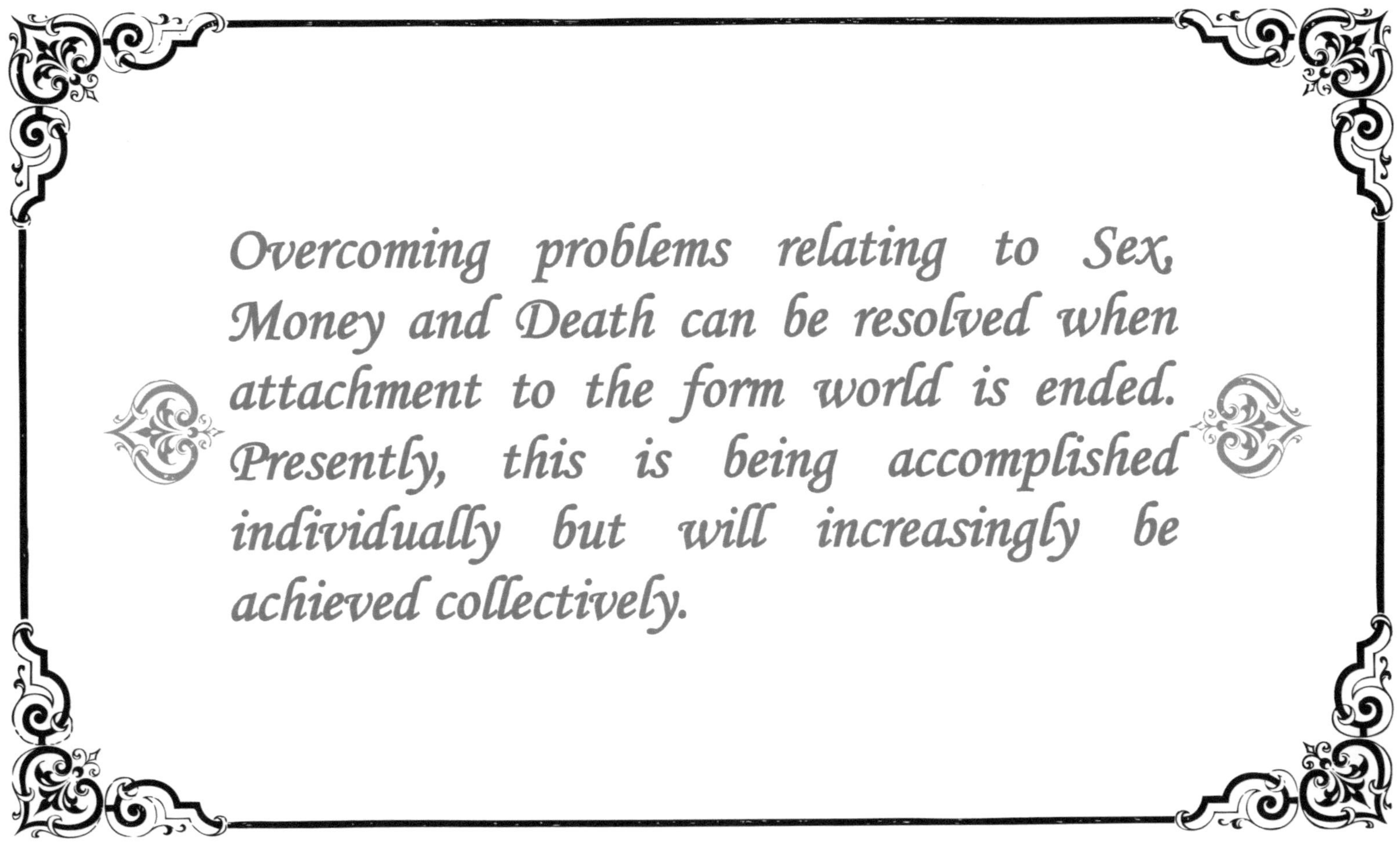

Overcoming problems relating to Sex, Money and Death can be resolved when attachment to the form world is ended. Presently, this is being accomplished individually but will increasingly be achieved collectively.

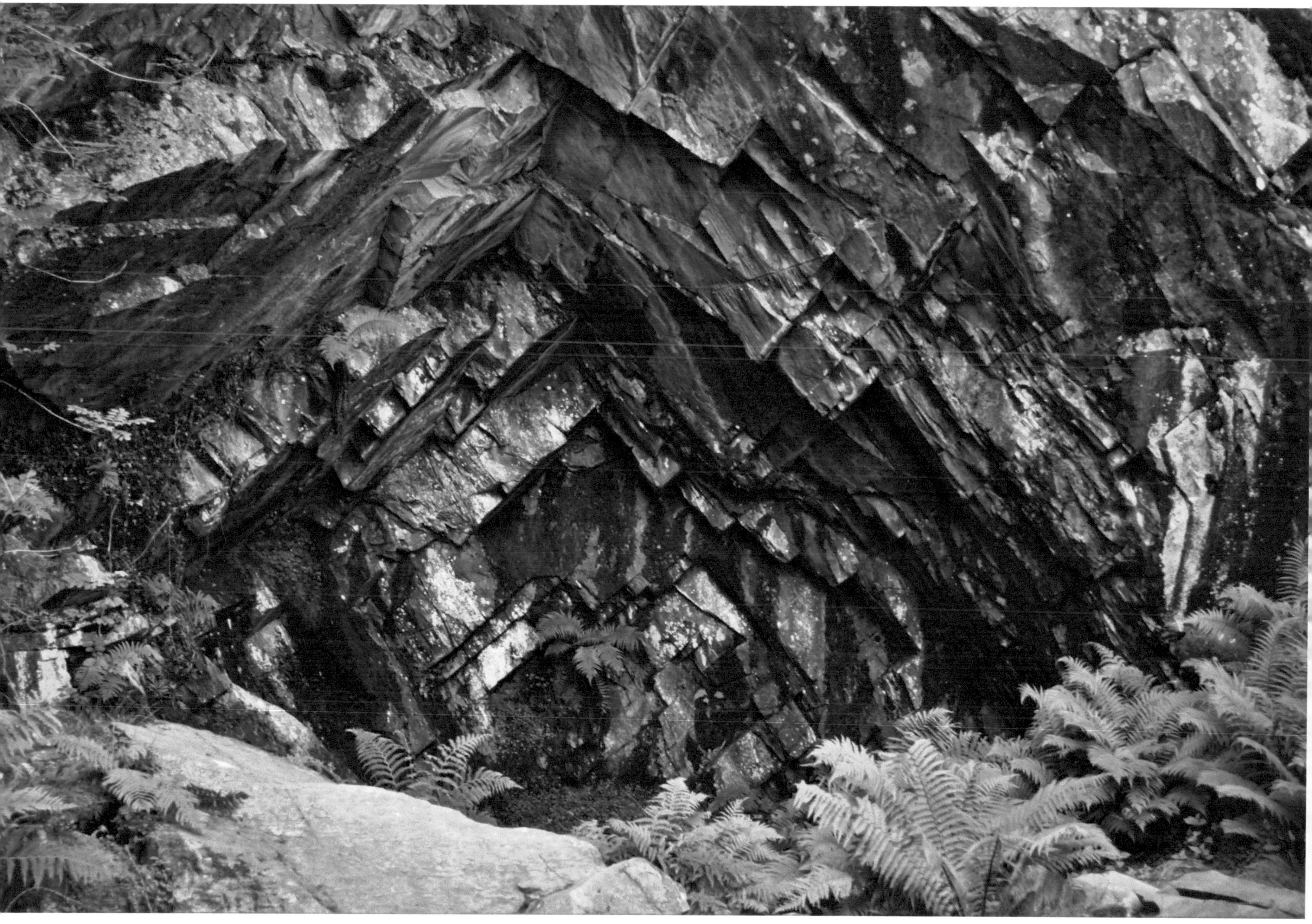

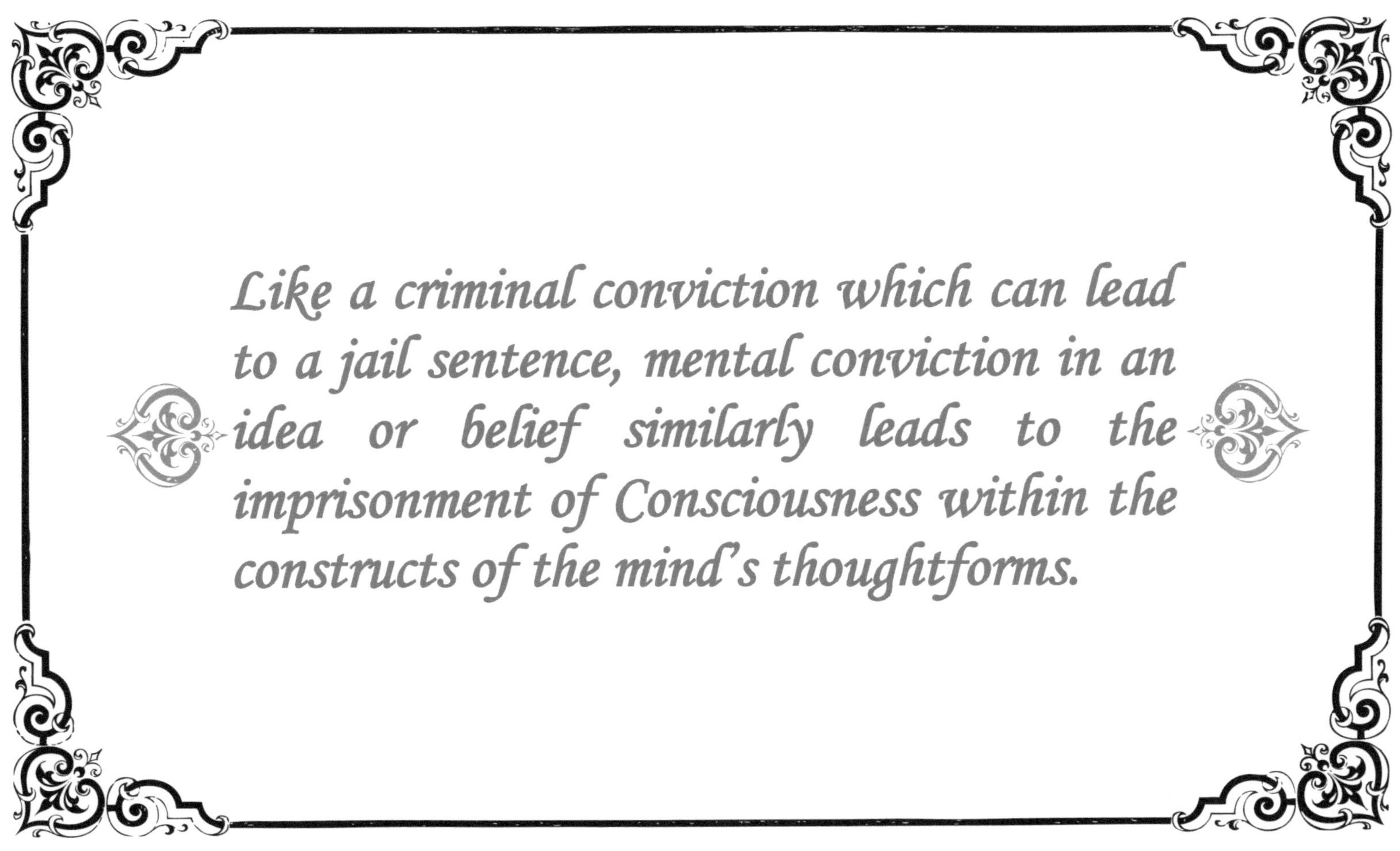

Like a criminal conviction which can lead to a jail sentence, mental conviction in an idea or belief similarly leads to the imprisonment of Consciousness within the constructs of the mind's thoughtforms.

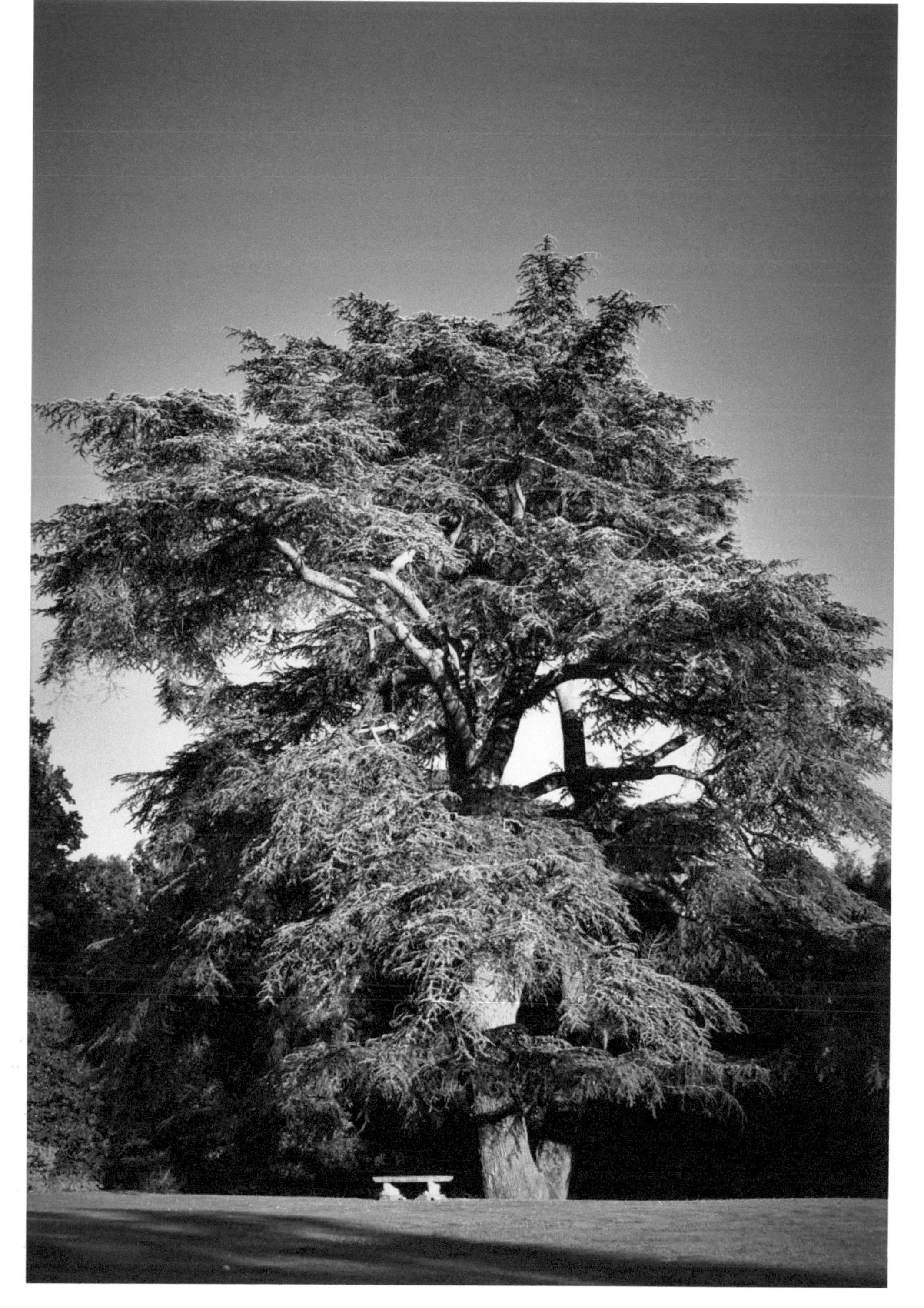

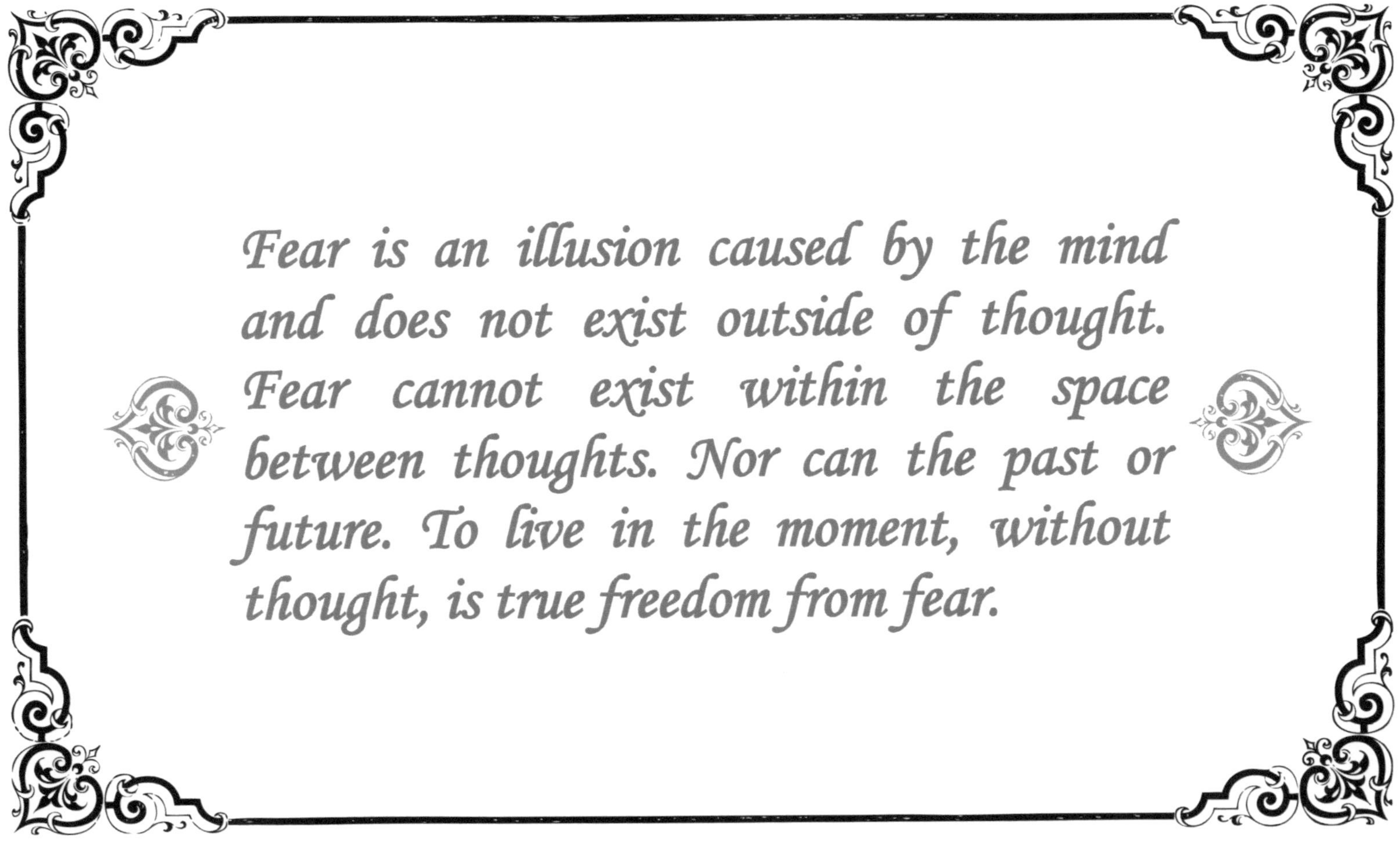

Fear is an illusion caused by the mind and does not exist outside of thought. Fear cannot exist within the space between thoughts. Nor can the past or future. To live in the moment, without thought, is true freedom from fear.

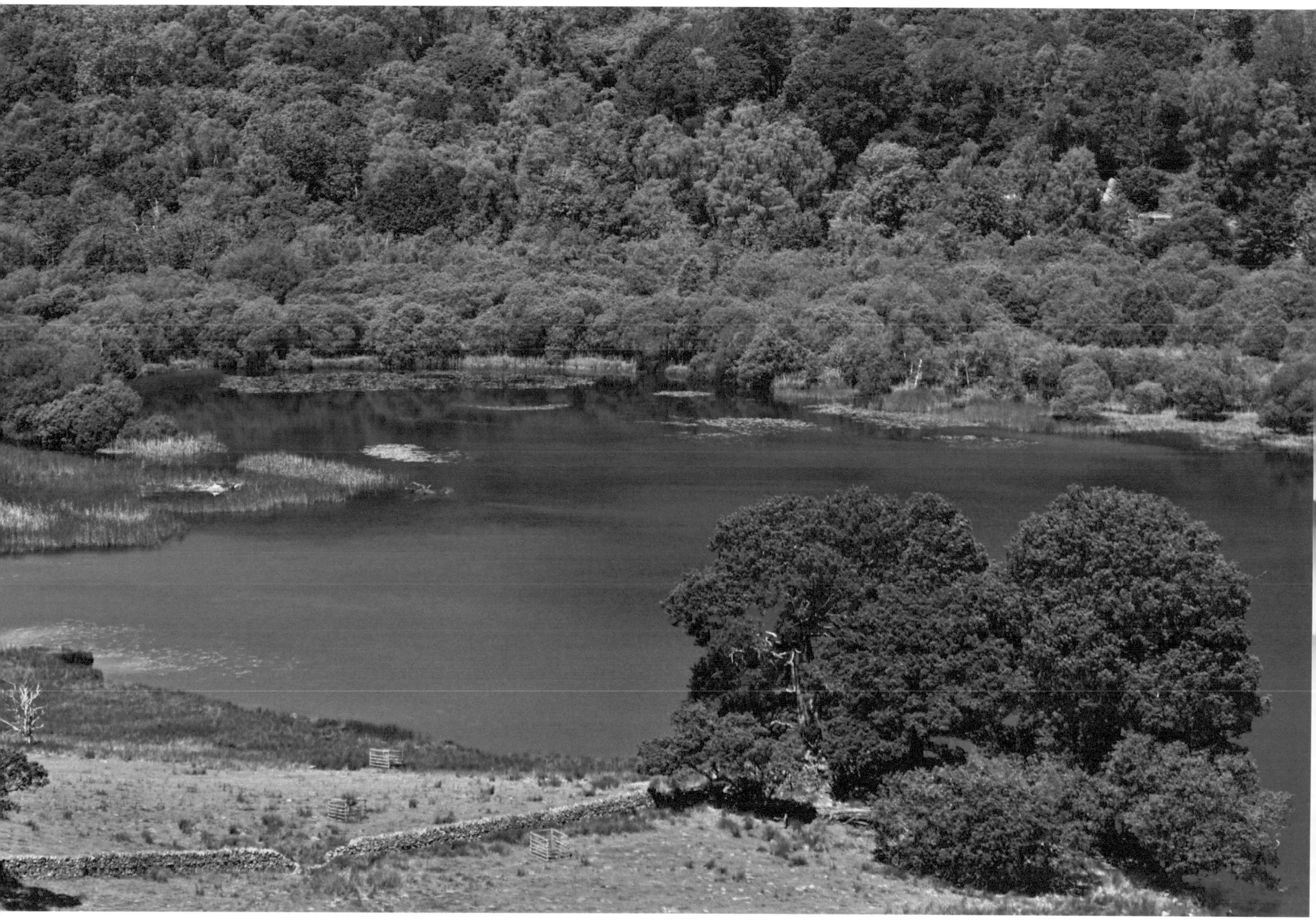

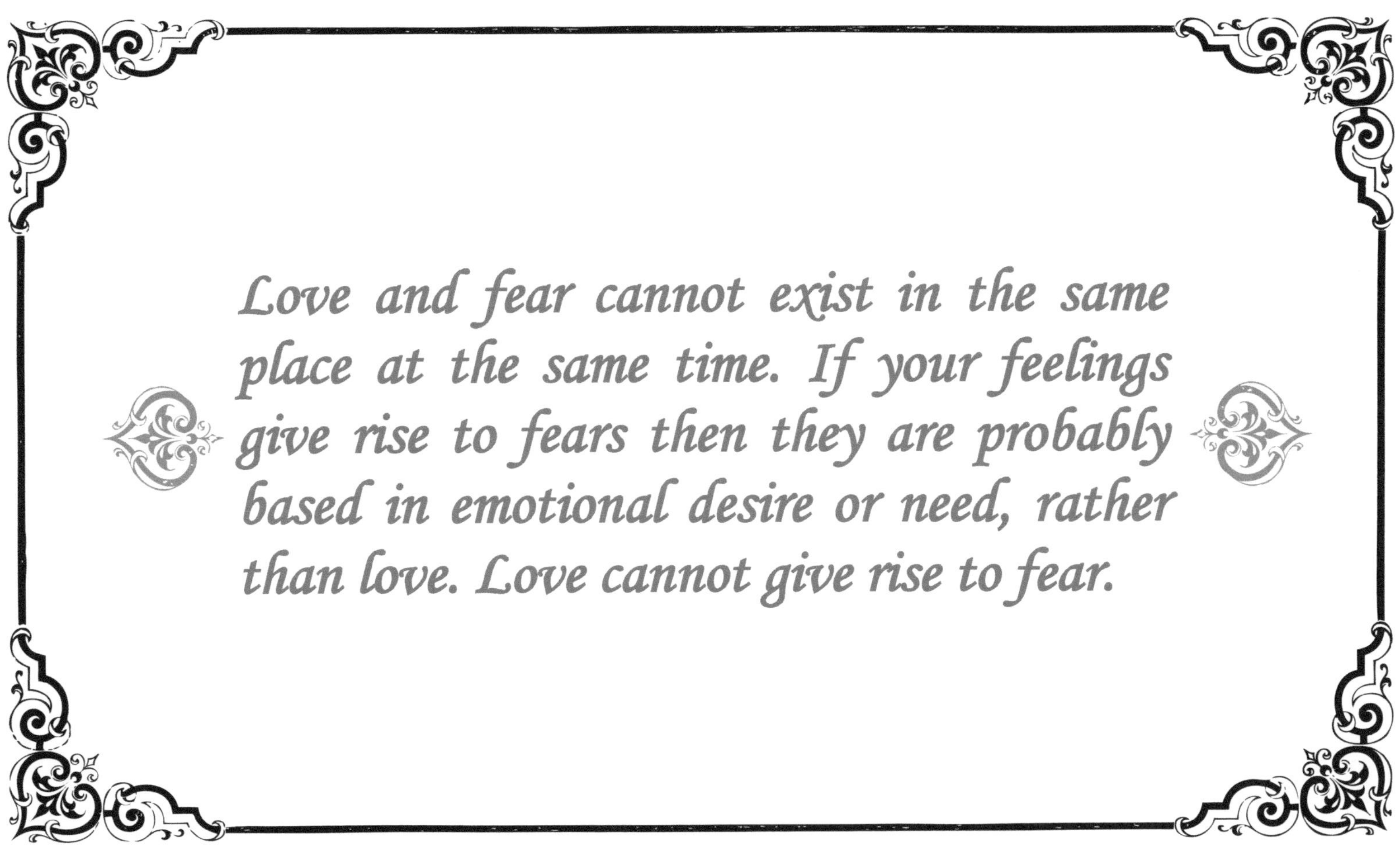

Love and fear cannot exist in the same place at the same time. If your feelings give rise to fears then they are probably based in emotional desire or need, rather than love. Love cannot give rise to fear.

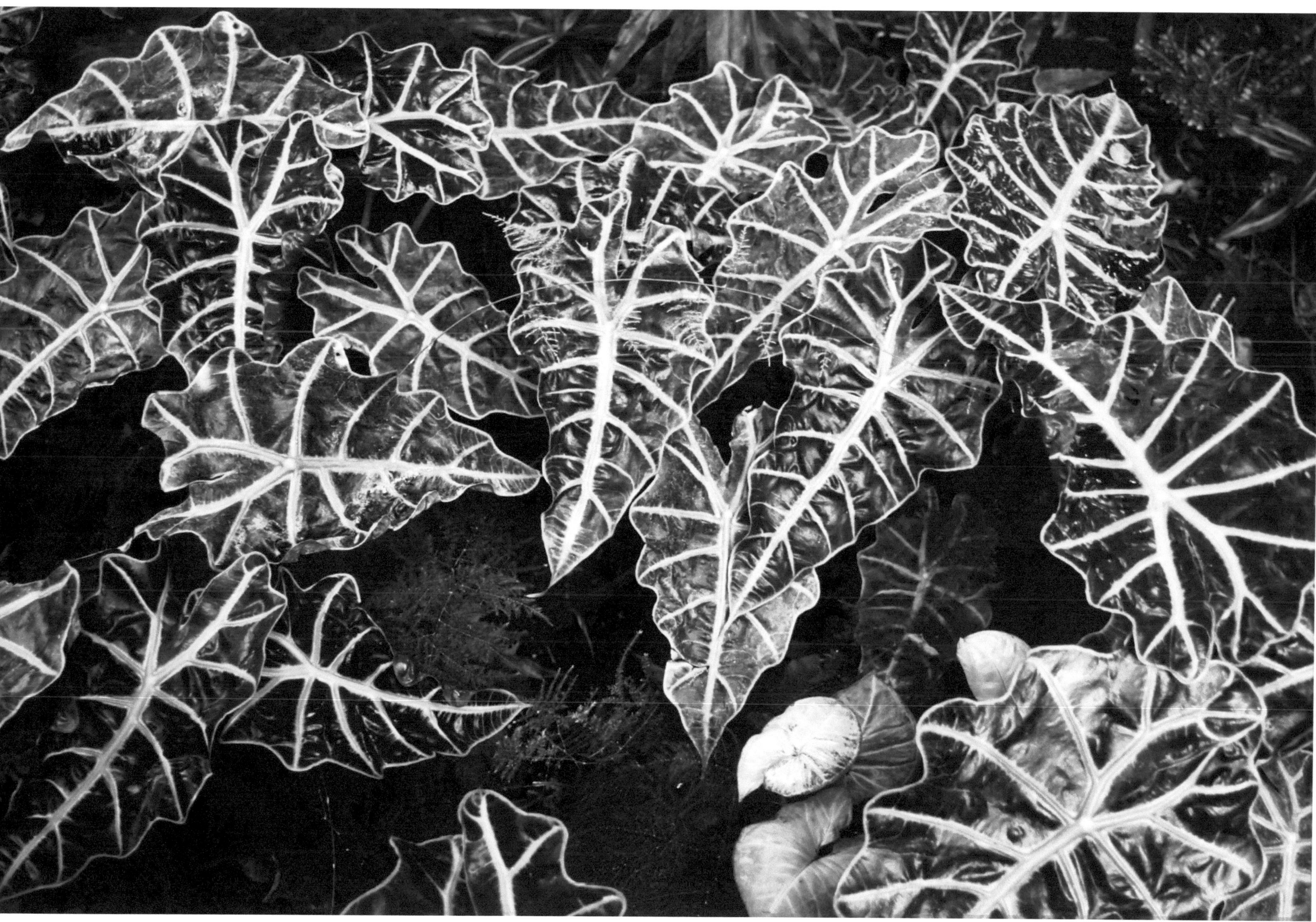

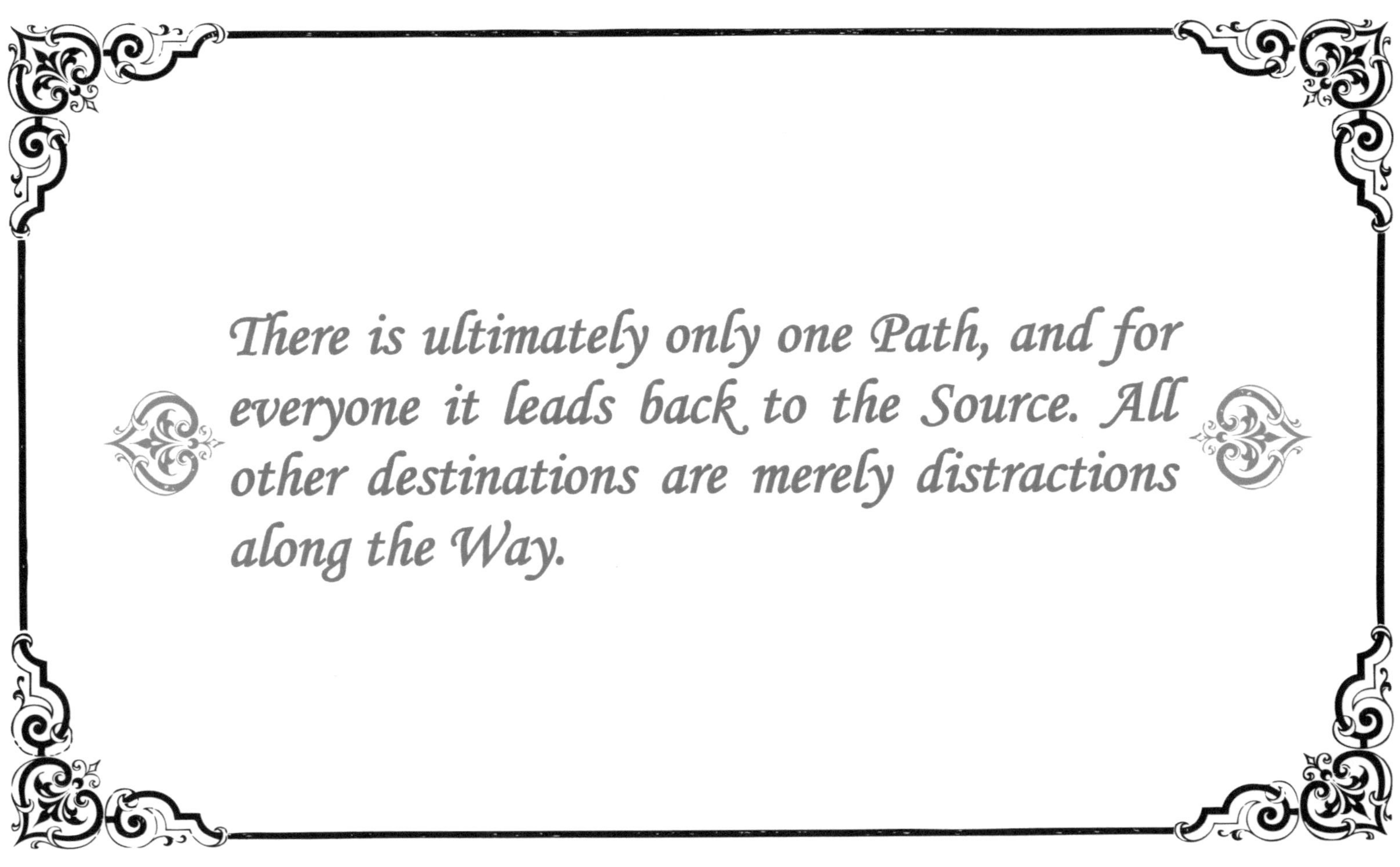

There is ultimately only one Path, and for everyone it leads back to the Source. All other destinations are merely distractions along the Way.

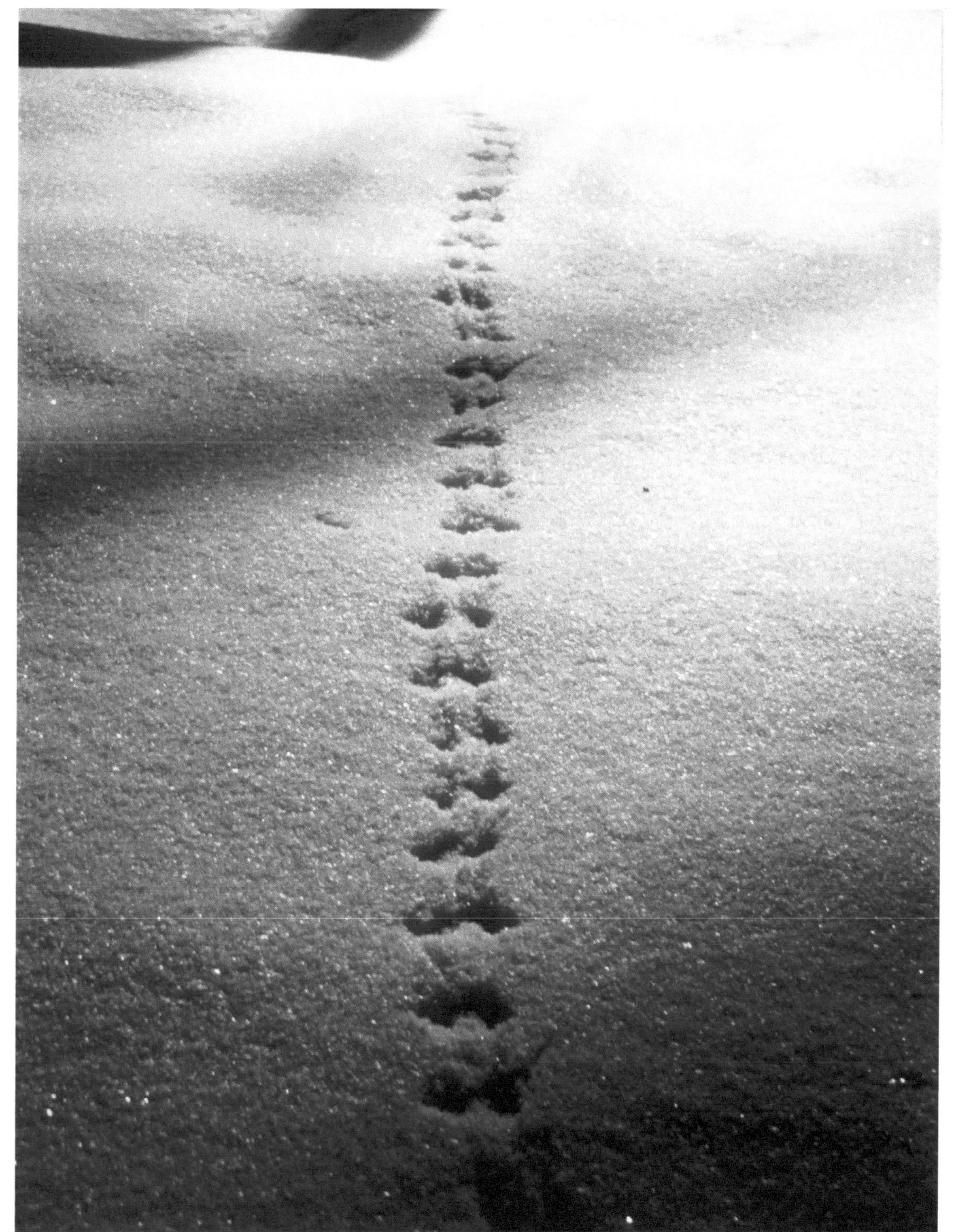

www.ingramcontent.com/pod-product-compliance
Lightning Source LLC
LaVergne TN
LVHW072328100826
845147LV00004B/661

9780987778246